A Taste of Murder

Also by Jo Grossman and Robert Weibezahl

A Second Helping of Murder: More Diabolically Delicious Recipes from Contemporary Mystery Writers

Jo Grossman and Robert Weibezahl are donating a portion of their profits from this book to From the Wholesaler to the Hungry, a national organization that helps cities across the country develop systematic programs to distribute nutritious, fresh produce to low-income adults and children.

A Taste of Murder

Diabolically Delicious Recipes
from Contemporary Mystery Writers

Jo Grossman   Robert Weibezahl

Poisoned Pen Press

Library of Congress Catalog Card Number: 2003110516

ISBN: 1-59058-076-1

Poisoned Pen Press
6962 E. First Ave. Ste 103
Scottsdale, AZ 85251
www.poisonedpenpress.com
info@poisonedpenpress.com

Printed in the United States of America

Cover Design: J.J. Smith-Moore
Interior Design: The Printed Page

Rights and Permissions

"Sole Hitchcock" from CHASEN'S: *Where Hollywood Dined, Recipes and Memories.* Copyright © 1996 by Betty Goodwin. Published by Angel City Press. Reprinted with permission of the publisher.

"Creole Seafood Gumbo" reprinted with permission from Brennan's Restaurant, New Orleans.

"Mrs. Hudson's Steak, Ale and Mushroom Pie" reprinted with permission from Sherlock Holmes Public House and Restaurant, London.

"Victoria Regina Chicken Pie" reprinted with permission from Sherlock Holmes Pub-Restaurant, Carmel, California.

"Brown's Hotel Afternoon Tea Scones" reprinted with permission from 1837, Brown's Hotel, London.

For my father, who introduced me to Sherlock Holmes, and my mother, who introduced me to Betty Crocker.

J.G.

For my family—and it's no mystery why.

R.W.

$\mathcal{A}$CKNOWLEDGMENTS

$\mathcal{A}$ project such as this one, by its very definition, is a collaborative effort, and we would like to thank all those who in one way or another helped us—with contacts, leads, research, suggestions, and moral support.

Our many angels from the publishing world included the publicists, editors, agents, and booksellers who put us in touch with contributors. Our thanks to Jane Beirn, Paddy Calistro, Mih-Ho Cha, Marie Coolman, Cassie Dendurent, Jeanine Johnson Flaherty, Andrea Bass Glickson, Jeannie Kaufman, Laura Leonard, Sara Narins, Jane Parritt, Sally Rauber, Ray Roberts, Danielle Robinson, Dana Schwartz, Charlotte Sheedy, Jennifer Suitor, Linda Urban, Toni Werbell, and Lisa Wright. If two publicists may be singled out, we must put in on record that the unflagging efforts of Mary Beth Gibson and Susan Richman were integral to our success. Ladies, you have our undying gratitude.

Tamara Asseyev was there at the start, and provided our first important "break." Three "non-mystery" writers, Mary Pat Kelly, Jo-Ann Mapson, and Lee Smith kindly put us in touch with some of their crime-writing comrades, and we thank them for crossing over into our world and offering their enthusiastic support. Betty Froelich expertly tested many recipes and was our consummate source on all this things culinary.

Many members of the Mystery Writers of America and Sisters in Crime did their part in helping disseminate word about the project, and we particularly thank Michael Jahn and Janice Steinberg. The wondrous on-line denizens of DorothyL provided some very useful information, as did friends and colleagues Judy Chase, Amy Cooper, Kathy Kamiya, Jacqueline Olds, and Fran Roy. And Susan Self, who supplied us with a treasure trove of research (unpaid!), deserves special acknowledgment.

Thanks to everyone at Dell, including our editors Danielle Perez and Jacquie Miller, the book's designer, Lynn Newmark, and our diligent copy editor, Kathy Lord, who caught all those pesky mistakes and made us look good. And very special thanks for our agent, Gareth Eserksy, who embraced this project with enthusiasm and helped shepherd it way beyond our initial expectations.

And while we thank them last, our foremost thanks go to the many generous mystery writers who contributed their recipes to the cause. We found ourselves in the enviable position of having more recipes than we needed and the equally *unenviable* position of having to choose those that could not be included. Each and every one of you is still part of the spirit of *A Taste of Murder*.

Contents

Introduction

First Instincts

Choose Your Poison

The Pot Thickens

Dressed to Kill

Kneadless Violence

Quick and Painless

Pasta Mortem

Something's Fishy

Fowl Play

Secret Meat-ings

No Place To Meat

Faithful Sidekicks

Revenge Is Sweet

Just Desserts

A Feast of Food and Felonies

$\mathcal{F}$ood has been a part of the crime novel since time immemorial (okay, maybe not *that* far back), so it seemed only natural that there should be a cookbook that would link those two indisputable pleasures—a good mystery and a good meal. As the idea for *A Taste of Murder* began to take shape, we knew that it needed to be more than just a compendium that cataloged the bountiful dinners of Nero Wolfe or the number of times Miss Marple has tea. This book would celebrate the tradition of food in mysteries, of course, but we also wanted it to be up-to-date, honoring some of today's most talented writers. Surely some of them cook, we pondered. And all of them eat. Why not gather the recipes for their favorite dishes into a cookbook that no true mystery fan would be able to resist? So we sent out feelers, exploited every tenuous connection we could think of, pestered publicists and editors, and tapped into the wonderful network of mystery writers and fans, begging, borrowing and stealing with abandon, until we compiled the collection you now have before you.

So what exactly is this elusive, undeniable connection between mystery fiction and food? On the most elementary level, of course, each provides its own particular form of sustenance to body or mind—or perhaps body or *soul* to the truly passionate, for it would seem that the diehard mystery fan would happily forego a meal or two to curl up with a volume of mayhem and deceit. But there must be an even stronger link, we felt, because you just don't find food playing such a central role in other fictional genres—does anyone ever eat in a science fiction novel? It cannot be a coincidence that two of the words we most often use to describe mysteries—*hard-boiled* and *cozy*—derive from food and drink.

There is such a venerable history of dining and death. From the earliest days, when a birthday dinner proved a pivotal event in Wilkie Collins' *The Moonstone*, purveyors of the art of the crime novel have been peppering their plots with things to eat—and things to avoid eating. Meals as social gatherings suit the writer who likes the idea of knocking off a guest or two, thereby inciting a professional or amateur detective—invariably present at the scene—to immediate action. These exercises in domestic detection can take place in palatial English country homes, chic New York apartments, or hallowed institutes of higher learning—all places where there never seems to be much to do other than eat and drink anyway.

Even as the body count mounts, readers can gobble up the details of these feasts and learn a bit about a particular time or place, because food provides great anthropological evidence. Writing about a certain part of the country, or another country all together, an author can spice up a narrative with references to regional foods (they eat *that*?) and make his or her home turf a bit more inviting for fans. In this regard, there is a marked difference between the foods featured in American crime novels and those in their British counterparts, and a vast difference in the manner and places in which they are served as well. Whereas the Brits enjoy a weekend-long house party, Yanks go more for a nice cocktail party where the guests are entertained but then expected to leave (if they're still alive). Charming old pubs are replaced by dark, usually seedy bars on this side of the Pond. They have the elegant tradition of afternoon tea, we have the market cornered on greasy spoons. We've noticed, too, that while American cops have earned a bad rep for consuming great quantities of coffee and doughnuts and other less-than-healthy food, English policemen (at least in mysteries) are all business and never seem to eat.

There are two murder weapons closely associated with food—poison and the knife. Poison is the preferred weapon of those who eschew violence and gore and, in these days of increasingly graphic crime novels, could almost be viewed as genteel. It is, of course, best administered in food or drink, so the wily mystery writer who chooses this method for disposing of the victim must put a lot of prandial activity into the plot. As Carlotta Oglethorpe has written in *Murder Ink*,

> *There are some foods in mysteries it's never safe to trust. Dover sole, baked or poached. Porridge. Ladyfingers. Any cream sauce. Eggs, unless they're hard-boiled. Chocolates, if they're given as a present. Warm milk. And, of course, any sort of spirits. The Case of the Deadly Decanter has been written at least a hundred times, and there's probably a fiend out there typing up another one right now. When analyzed, the sediment always contains enough poison to fell a hippopotamus.*

Death by stabbing, on the other hand, is a major commitment, especially if you need to go steal a knife from the kitchen, which could leave a trail of evidence. Plus you'll need to contend with the cook, who will be either temperamental (French), imperious (English), or surly (American), although there is the advantage of throwing suspicion his or her way. When a knife or poison is involved, the cook is invariably a suspect, but rarely guilty. Where would be the mystery in that?

Other than as weapon (or as alibi), there is another way that food seems to be cropping up in mysteries with increasing frequency. As comfort. "Have something to eat," Diane Mott Davidson's sleuthing caterer Goldy Schulz has been heard to say. "Food heals all messes." Many of the recipes in *A Taste of Murder* are fashioned along these lines, with our contributors sharing the foods that make them happy after a hard day of writing, or soothe their tired detectives when an investigation just doesn't seem to be going their way. These dishes, we hope, will offer comfort and delight readers as well.

We find more than a kernel of truth in an observation made by Jeanine Larmoth in *Murder on the Menu*:

> *Hidden within each mystery reader is a gourmet; guiding each stroke of the writer's pen is a chef of chef d'oeuvres. If mysteries contain menus and recipes for murder, happily they contain menus and recipes for meals as well. Between shudders of fear and apprehension at a past or coming crime are delightful islands where the principal consideration is the next dish, and the shudders are solely pleasurable.*

There have always been mystery novels where food is as much the point as the crime—Rex Stout's Nero Wolfe books leap first to mind—but the avalanche of "culinary" mysteries being published today seems unstoppable. As Jeff Siegel has pointed out in *Gourmet* magazine, it's sometimes impossible to tell a detective without a menu. Diane Mott Davidson, Robert B. Parker, Mary Daheim, Camilla Crespi, Ellen Hart, Valerie S. Malmont, Tamar Myers, Lou Jane Temple, Michael Bond, Peter King, Joanne Pence, Katherine Hall Page, Phyllis Richman, and Nancy Pickard, who is continuing Virginia Rich's Eugenia Potter series, are just a handful of the mystery writers who infuse their work with the pleasures of good cooking. Many of these fine writers have generously contributed to *A Taste of Murder*.

As mystery fans and cooks alike, we've both discovered ways to blend the two. Bob can occasionally be found turning the pages of a mystery novel while stirring a recipe for a favorite sauce or stew. Jo, for her part, opened The Mystery Café in the Berkshires (MA) where customers could enjoy good food and good mysteries under one roof. Since the café has recently shut its doors, we've included one of its most-craved desserts in here for all to savor.

One last explanation for the mystery-food connection? Kathy Kamiya, an inveterate mystery reader and good friend, has suggested that it may stem from the fact that cooking shares something basic with solving crime. She may be onto something. When you cook, whether from a recipe or not, you must assemble the ingredients in the same way that you might clues. One step leads to another and the solution—the final dish—cannot be reached without every element put into place in its proper order. One false move and the whole enterprise could come to naught. And, of course, the satisfaction that comes from solving a tricky mystery is tantamount to sitting down to a well-prepared meal.

A Taste of Murder is a casual companion for mystery readers who like to cook or cooks who like to read mysteries (no, these are not the same thing). Whether you want to whip up the favorite dish of your favorite writer (or his or her fictional detective), put together a mystery-inspired meal, or just sit in bed on a cold winter's night and read about food-loving sleuths, there's enough nourishment here to feed both the imagination and the belly. We promise both good food and good company.

But please remember: Gluttony is one of the seven deadly sins. Murder is not.

FIRST INSTINCTS

Jalapeños à la Frontera
ALLANA MARTIN

*L*ike Spanglish, the speedball mix of Spanish and English that is the language of the Texas-Mexico borderland, this appetizer recipe combines American and Mexican foods, all of which are favorites of Texana Jones.

> 1 medium can whole pickled jalapeño peppers (*)
> ¾ cup sharp cheddar cheese, grated
> 1 cup buttermilk
> ½ cup flour
> Oil

Drain the jalapeños and dry with paper towels. Leave the stems on the peppers. Make a small lengthwise slice in each pepper and scrape out the core and seeds. Stuff the peppers generously with the grated cheese. (Do all the peppers before going on to the next step.) Holding the pepper by the stem, dip each in buttermilk and then in flour. Place on a plate and chill at least 30 minutes in the refrigerator to set the coating. (This may be done a day ahead and chilled overnight.) Heat enough oil to cover peppers; add 1 or 2 of the coated peppers and fry until golden. Drain on paper towels and serve.

*Helpful hint: Fresh jalapeños can be used but are extremely hot. If you don't know where to find whole pickled jalapeños in your area, contact Vitore Foods of Laredo, Texas, (956) 726-3633, to learn who near you carries their La Costeña brand.)

Allana Martin is the author of the Texana Jones mystery series which includes *Death of An Evangelista, Death of A Saint Maker* and *Death of A Healing Woman.*

Armadillo Eggs

MAUREEN TAN

*I*n the suspense novel, *a.k.a. Jane*, British MI-5 agent Jane Nichols discovers there's more to Savannah, Georgia than red mud, winding river roads, moss-hung trees, and plantation homes. She finds murder, intrigue, love, and food—lots of wonderful food.

Wonderful restaurants reflect the richness, diversity, and quirkiness of Savannah's culture. The food at BillyBob's on historic East River Street is a touch of down-home cooking for an author who has lived the past two decades in south central Illinois and points west. As Jane Nichols struggles to bring an international terrorist to justice, she and her team take time out to dine on barbecue ribs and armadillo eggs.

Every time I reread that particular scene, my mouth waters.

> 2 jalapeño peppers
> 1 8-ounce package cream cheese
> Bread crumbs
> A wash made from egg white and a little water

Slice a jalapeño pepper into 4 to 6 long slices and remove the seeds. Roll a slice into a ball to form the "yolk." Place it in the middle of a ball of cream cheese about the size of a small egg; press in place. Roll the resulting "egg" in bread crumbs and brush with the egg white wash.

Important: Place in a refrigerator or freezer until very firm. Deep-fry until golden brown. Serve hot, with salsa and sliced lemon on the side.

Makes 8 to 12 "eggs."

Maureen Tan is the author of *a.k.a. Jane* and *Run Jane Run*.

Sympathy for the Deviled Eggs

(The Cold Appetizer From Hell)

JERRILYN FARMER

*I*n *Sympathy for the Devil*, Madeline Bean, caterer to the stars, and her partner Wesley have pulled off Hollywood's most outrageous A-list Halloween party for notorious producer Bruno Huntley, complete with an eerie fortune-teller who is astonishing and exotic cuisine that is totally cool. Before long, Bruno is thrashing and writhing on the dance floor. Just one problem: he's not standing up. And soon he's not even breathing.

When Wesley is arrested for murder, Madeline begins to unravel a mystery that leads her back to the early days of California, and a long forgotten curse that may still haunt the wealthy Los Feliz neighborhood to this day. Perhaps. But Madeline, wit intact, manages to bring things bumping back to the present. She uncovers a trail of offbeat nineties characters, one of whom has cooked up a devil of a murder—right in Madeline's own kitchen.

> 12 large eggs, hard boiled (or cozy) and peeled
> ¼ cup mayonnaise
> 1 tablespoon ground cumin
> 1 tablespoon Dijon mustard
> ½ teaspoon salt
> 1 jalapeño pepper, seeded and finely chopped
> Red chiles, ground
> Fresh cilantro, snipped

The first step may be performed with a dagger: Cut the eggs in half, lengthwise. Next, using the finesse of a cat burglar, ease out the yolks and reserve the whites. In a medium bowl, mash the yolks mercilessly with a fork, mixing in the mayonnaise, cumin, mustard, salt and the jalapeño pepper. Clean getaway? Not yet. First, fill the egg whites with the egg-yolk mixture, heaping ever so lightly. Then hide the clues: Sprinkle with ground red chiles, and garnish with the snipped cilantro.

Caterer/sleuth Madeline Bean's tip: Presentation can elevate the humble egg to gourmet status. Place several dozen eggs on your most beautiful platter and create a lovely border all around with full sprigs of fresh cilantro. Make plenty. One should never underestimate the attraction of a great deviled egg.

Serves 12 modestly hungry accomplices.

Jerrilyn Farmer's caterer/sleuth, Madeline Bean, can be found in *Sympathy For the Devil* and *Immaculate Reception*.

Wayne Caruso's Sweet Bread Spread

JAQUELINE GIRDNER

Okay, I had the bread spread that Kate Jasper's significant other had created. (It seemed only fair, since I created him.) And my husband was gobbling it up, licking the spoon, the blender, and the cook. But did I have a credible plot? Poor old Soy Tofu. Who would want to kill the Lord of the Bland? The Blender! Its facade was quiet, domestic, even submissive, until the wrong button was pushed, and then its blades whirled mercilessly! But I needed more: the sweet romance of maple and vanilla; the tart irony of lemon, the gritty insanity of peanut butter. And finally, the suspense of the fruit conserves. Which one to use? Ah, but only you, the reader, can solve this final mystery.

>   1 package light silken tofu
>   1 bottle fruit conserves
>   2 tablespoons maple syrup
>   2 tablespoons lemon juice
>   2 tablespoons vanilla extract
>   2 to 4 tablespoons peanut butter

Blend all ingredients in blender. Enjoy on bread or crackers.

Please note: No living soy beings were harmed in the making of this recipe.

Murder on the Astral Plane and *Death Hits the Fan* are two of Jaqueline Girdner's mystery novels.

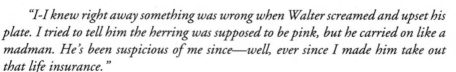

"I-I knew right away something was wrong when Walter screamed and upset his plate. I tried to tell him the herring was supposed to be pink, but he carried on like a madman. He's been suspicious of me since—well, ever since I made him take out that life insurance."

"What was the face amount on the policy?"

"A hundred thousand. But it carried a triple-indemnity clause in case he died by seafood."

—S.J. Perelman, *"Farewell, My Lovely Appetizer"*

Thea's Quick and Dirty Bluefish Pâté

KATE FLORA

*T*his recipe appears in my fourth Thea Kozak mystery, *An Educated Death*. Thea is a workaholic consultant, but she remembers the days when she used to have a life and entertain. In the midst of solving a mystery at a private school, she finds the headmistress' secretary in a funk because she has a crowd coming to her house for a holiday party and no food prepared. Thea reels off a whole list of quick and dirty party foods, including the following:

In food processor, combine:

> ⅓ to ½ pound smoked bluefish
> 8 ounces cream cheese
> 1 tablespoon horseradish
> Juice of one lemon

Process until smooth. Sample. Adjust seasoning to taste. Andre, the Maine police detective who is the new man in Thea's life, likes enough horseradish to clear the sinuses. If too thick, thin with milk or cream. Serve with crackers or cucumber slices. You never know when a hungry cop may drop by....

After working for the Attorney General of Maine specializing in child protection cases, Kate Flora turned to mystery writing. The Thea Kozak series includes *Death in Paradise*, *An Educated Death* and *Death at the Wheel*.

Sausage-Cheese Appetizer

BILL CRIDER

One of my characters, Sheriff Dan Rhodes, doesn't do much cooking. For him a bologna sandwich is a stretch. But he does know how to make one appetizer that's so easy even he can't mess it up. Here it is:

> 1 pound hot venison sausage
> (if you don't have venison, any hot sausage will do)
> 1 pound mild cheddar cheese, shredded
> 3 cups biscuit mix

Crumble the cooked sausage into a large bowl, add the cheese, and mix well. Blend biscuit mix into the sausage-cheese mixture with a pastry blender. Shape into walnut-size balls and place on ungreased cookie sheets. Bake at 450 degrees for 10 minutes, and you'll have about 9 dozen great appetizers. If you can't eat that many, put the ones that are left over into moisture-proof freezer containers. When you want to eat them, heat at 350 degrees until they get warm.

Bill Crider is the author of the Anthony Award-nominated short story "How I Found a Cat, Lost True Love, and Broke the Bank at Monte Carlo," and the Sheriff Dan Rhodes novels, *Winning Can Be Murder* and *Too Late to Die*, which won the Anthony Award as best first mystery novel.

Capunatina alla Fortunati

JANE RUBINO

*I*n the debut Austen/Cardenas mystery, *Death of a DJ*, Lieutenant Cardenas is invited to Sunday dinner with Cat's family and withstands the scrutiny of the Fortunati brothers with considerably more stamina than he endures the unrelenting procession of food. The food comes in courses, on and on and on, and keeps coming long after Victor Cardenas has the will or inclination to eat.

Olive oil (the best quality)
2 large eggplants
2 large onions, chopped
4 stalks celery, chopped
6 large cloves garlic, sliced
1 large can (2 ½ pounds) chopped tomatoes
1 jar (7 ounce) large capers, drained and rinsed

1 large can pitted black olives, drained, rinsed, quartered
1 bunch fresh basil, remove several leaves for garnish, chop the rest
Salt and pepper, to taste
2 tablespoons sugar
3 tablespoons balsamic vinegar
¼ cup dark raisins and
½ cup toasted pignoli (optional)

Preparation time: The eggplant will need to drain for about 2 hours; after that, the preparation is about ½ hour. The capunatina may be prepared earlier in the day, or even a day in advance.

Peel the eggplant and chop in 1-inch cubes. Place in a large colander and salt liberally; let stand 1 hour to allow liquid to drain off. Resalt and let stand another hour. Rinse and squeeze between paper towels.

In a large skillet, heat ¼ cup olive oil and sauté the onion and celery for 3 minutes; add garlic and sauté another two minutes, or until the garlic is golden and translucent. Add the canned tomatoes, capers, olives, chopped basil, salt and pepper to taste (¼ teaspoon each should do it), reduce heat, and simmer 10 minutes. While this is simmering heat ⅓ cup olive oil in a separate skillet, sauté the eggplant until soft (8-10 minutes). (This may have to be done using 2 skillets, dividing the eggplant cubes between them.) You may need to add more olive oil, since eggplant tends to absorb it. When the eggplant is tender, use a slotted spoon to transfer it to the tomato-vegetable mixture. Combine the sugar and vinegar, add to skillet, and mix all the ingredients thoroughly while continuing to simmer for another 3 to 5 minutes. Turn off the heat. If you are using raisins and pignoli, they are added at this point.

Transfer to a serving platter and garnish with whole basil leaves; serve with focaccia. Although some recipes say that capunatina may be served cold, it is best warm or at room temperature. You may prepare it several hours in advance and leave it out, covered with wax paper until ready to serve.

Bonupitittu!

Jane Rubino's Cat Austen/Victor Cardenas mysteries include *Death of a DJ*, *Fruitcake,* and *Cheat the Devil.*

CHOOSE YOUR POISON

Trials and Bibulations

*H*ard-drinking detectives are as much a part of crime novels as poison, revolvers and the ironclad alibi. It's hard to think of any hard-boiled private eye worth his or her salt who *doesn't* drink. Most of them would feel at sea if their investigations did not allow them to frequent a seedy bar or two for a shot of whiskey or a glass of beer.

The cocktail is something else entirely. These potent concoctions signal a degree of refinement and class, and, not surprisingly, the cocktail drinkers among fictional crime-solvers are generally well-heeled, if not upper class. Crime fiction from the thirties, forties and fifties is rife with these ever-cheerful partakers.

Nick and Nora Charles in Dashiell Hammett's *The Thin Man* come immediately to mind, and there is hardly a page in that classic that does not find Nick, Nora, or one of their cohorts having a drink or nursing a hangover (*"How about a drop of something to cut the phlegm,"* Nick asks after a night on the town.) Sadly, Hammett is a bit vague about what all these people are drinking.

Picking up the jigger where Hammett dropped it, Frances and Richard Lockridge created Mr. and Mrs. North, less wealthy and less acerbic incarnations of Nick and Nora. In their first adventure, *The Norths Meet Murder,* Pam North wants to throw a party in the vacant apartment above their own. After mollifying her tired, reluctant husband, Jerry, with a Tom Collins ("it's *the warmest October in sixty-eight years*"), they ascend to the upper floor of their Greenwich Village brownstone, where they discover the body of a murdered man. The investigation is afoot and the liquor flows freely. Even the cops in this series enjoy their cocktails—while on duty!

> *The Norths were home, and at cocktails, which they urged on Weigand and Mullins. Weigand said that, of course, they were on duty—Mullins looked very unhappy—and that they would be very glad of cocktails. Mullins beamed, his beam grew when Mr. North, after a quick look, suggested he might prefer rye. Mullins did prefer rye.*

And the culprit is finally snatched, of course, at another cocktail party staged for just that reason.

Mr. and Mrs. North Tom Collins

2 to 2 ½ ounces gin
1 to 2 teaspoons sugar
½ to 1 ounce freshly squeezed lemon juice
Iced club soda
1 slice lemon (optional)
1 slice orange (optional)
1 maraschino cherry (optional)

Shake the gin, sugar, and lemon juice well with ice. Strain into tall 14-ounce glass, half-filled with ice. Add the soda. Stir. Add the lemon, orange, and/or cherry as preferred.

In Ellery Queen's venerable *Calamity Town,* a cocktail is at the center of the murder plot. At a New Year's party, an out-of-town guest falls prey to a Manhattan laced with arsenic. The only problem: It wasn't intended for her. Or was it?

Calamity Town Manhattan

(Hold the Arsenic)

1 ½ to 2 ounces blended whiskey
½ ounce sweet vermouth
1 dash bitters (optional)
1 maraschino cherry

Stir the whiskey, vermouth, and bitters well with ice. Strain into pre-chilled cocktail glass. Add cherry.

During our own gilded age, Lawrence Sanders' irrepressible bon vivant lawyer Archie McNally seems to spend about as much time drinking at the Pelican Club or one of Palm Beach's other watering holes as he does working. McNally appreciates the finer things in life—expensive cars, fine wines, and world class art. And, of course, a good martini. He apparently acquired his patrician tastes from McNally *père*:

> *The senior McNally would go through the ritual of mixing a pitcher (not too large) of gin martinis. I know it is fashionable to demand* dry *martinis; the drier the better. Some insist on a mixture of eight or ten parts gin to one of vermouth. In fact, I know fanatics who believe having an unopened bottle of vermouth somewhere in the neighborhood is sufficient.*
>
> *But my father is an ardent traditionalist, and his martinis were mixed in the classic formula: three parts gin, one part vermouth. The result was so odd and unusual that I found it enjoyable. The sire did relax his stern standards to the extent of using olives stuffed with a bit of jalapeño pepper.*
>
> —from *McNally's Secret*

Though first and foremost an American invention (Lord Peter Wimsey denounces the newfangled custom of cocktails before dinner), the diligent reader will no doubt find a few British whodunits where the practice has been embraced. Let us not forget, after all, that James Bond likes his *vodka* Martini shaken, not stirred.

Tres Navarre's South Texas Margarita
RICK RIORDAN

*M*y Tres Navarre PI series is set in San Antonio, so Tex-Mex food and drink are very dear to me. My character Tres is, among other things, a former bartender, and the recipe below was taken from a real-life friend of mine who tended bar in South Texas for many years.

> *The perfect margarita should be on the rocks, not frozen. Fresh squeezed limes, never a mixer. Cointreau rather than triple sec. No tequila but Herradura Anejo, a brand that until a few years ago was only available across the border. All three ingredients in equal proportions. And without salt on the rim it might as well be a daiquiri.*
>
> —from *Big Red Tequila*

Step 1:
Mix:

> 1 cup Herradura Anejo tequila
> 1 cup Cointreau
> 1 cup fresh-squeezed lime juice
> 2 cups ice cubes
> 1 fresh-squeezed lemon

Step 2:
Take the lemon rind and rub the rim of a 12-ounce glass so it is barely moist, then dip the rim into margarita salt.

Step 3:
Add ice cubes to the glass and strain in the mixture.

Step 4:
¡Salud!

Rick Riordan's books include *The Widower's Two-Step* and *Big Red Tequila*.

Neil Hamel's Jell-O Shots

JUDITH VAN GIESON

"One of the best ways not to feel like a lawyer on those days when I don't want to feel like a lawyer is to mix up a batch of Jell-O shots and have the Kid over for dinner. I got home late, so he brought the dinner, sopapillas from Paco's, not as good as the sopapillas from Arriba Tacos in Santa Fe, but hot enough to remind you that you were in the state where people ask if they need a visa to visit and whether it's safe to drink the water. We sat on my deck slurping cool green Jell-O shots and eating red-hot sopapillas, but it wasn't doing a thing to lower my body's temperature...."
—from *The Wolf Path*

1 package lime Jell-O
1 cup hot water
1 cup cold tequila
Splash of triple sec
Slices of lime

Stir the cup of hot water and Jell-O together in a bowl until mixed. Add the tequila (Neil likes Cuervo Gold) and triple sec, and float lime slices on top. Put in refrigerator until it jells. Cut into cubes and serve in wineglasses, or let sit at room temperature until it is liquid enough to drink. Slurp slowly; they are strong.

Judith Van Gieson's mystery series, featuring Albuquerque PI Neil Hamel, includes *Ditch Rider*, *Parrot Blues*, and *The Other Side of Death*.

Electric Lemonade

PAULA L. WOODS

*I*n my first Detective Charlotte Justice mystery, *Inner City Blues*, I had fun playing with the concept of *blue* in all of it's permutations—the Marvin Gaye song used in the title, the LAPD's concept of a "thin blue line," and more you'll just have to read the book to find.

But when it came to blue food, I figured my options would be severely limited, until it was time for Charlotte to order a drink and I wrote the line, *The first sip of my Electric Lemonade was a soothing blue balm for my jangled nerves.*

And knew I had it made in the shade!

> 1 ½ ounces lemon vodka
> ¾ ounce blue curaçao
> 4 ounces fresh lemonade
> Lemon wheel to garnish

Pour the lemon vodka, blue curaçao, and lemonade in a tall glass and fill with ice cubes. Stir with a straw until well blended. Make a short slit halfway through the lemon wheel and place on rim of glass.

Serves 1.

Paula L. Woods is the author of *Inner City Blues*, a Charlotte Justice mystery, and editor of the Anthony and Macavity-nominated anthology *Spooks, Spies, and Private Eyes: Black Mystery, Crime, and Suspense Fiction of the 20th Century.*

Susan Silverman's Boiled Water
ROBERT B. PARKER

When invited to participate in this cookbook, Robert Parker kindly responded :

Since there is a Spenser cookbook in development, I guess I better not. But should you wish to be frivolous, you might wish to use Susan's recipe for boiled water, which follows:

Place 1 ½ cups of water in a small pot

Place over high heat

Check occasionally but do not watch.

After water bubbles vigorously, remove. Serve in a pretty cup with a squeeze of lemon and some Equal.

Among Robert B. Parker's many Spenser novels are *Hush Money, Ceremony* and *Valediction*.

THE POT THICKENS

Like a simmering sauce, the plot was beginning to thicken.

—Peter King, *The Gourmet Detective*

Flap Tucker's Golden Asparagus Soup

PHILLIP DEPOY

This soup recipe is found in *Easy*, the first book of my series featuring a Zen detective from Atlanta named Flap Tucker. Along with Dalliance Oglethorpe, who runs a nightclub on Ponce de Leon called Easy, he finds what he's looking for—people, objects, solutions— through a combination of genuine detective work and trance-state awareness of the facts. The soup is served at a fictional Tibetan place called The Golden Potala, which Flap Tucker frequents. It helps him concentrate.

> Chicken parts
> 6 cups of water (for stock)
> Asparagus spears (minus tips, cut up)
> Salt
> Fresh dill
> 1 bay leaf
> Fresh ground pepper
> Lemon wedge
> Garlic
> Red French non-Bordeaux wine   (Côtes du Rhône, Brouilly)
> Fresh chives

In 6 cups of salted water, boil the back, neck, and wing tips of a chicken you've cut up for the more substantial part of the meal (say, coq au vin.) While it boils, cut the tips and ends off a big fistful of asparagus stalks. Throw away the ends, and save the tips for a side dish (maybe with the coq au vin) or for another day. Cut the rest of the stalks into 1-inch pieces and toss them into the boiling stock pot. Continue boiling for 5 minutes, then reduce the heat to a fair simmer. Add fresh chopped dill, a bay leaf, one turn of the pepper mill, one squeeze of lemon, a knifepoint of garlic, and a healthy splash of a nice Côtes du Rhône or Brouilly. Cover the soup and simmer for a good hour or so while you drink half the bottle of wine. Save the remainder of the bottle to drink with the soup. When the soup is finished, carefully remove the bay leaf, back, neck, and wing tips from the stock so as not to leave any little pieces or bones. (Some choose to remove a little of the meat from the back and neck and return it to the stock—it's not a crime.) Just before serving the soup, chop up a few fresh chives and dash them onto the surface of the soup.

Serve with the rest of the wine and a little fresh bread. Just before the first taste, imagine winter in the Himalayas, at the top of the world—then sip and see how warm the world can be.

Phillip DePoy's Flap Tucker series includes *Easy*, *Too Easy* and *Easy As 1,2,3*.

Sydney Teague's Spinach Soup

ANNE UNDERWOOD GRANT

$\mathcal{M}$y protagonist is a single mom, as I was (am). When I would begin to get the guilts each winter when cold nights begged for home cooking, especially vegetables and something that would "stick" to my kids' ribs, I made up a "catchall" soup in honor of as many food groups as I could remember. I am particularly proud of the spinach in here because my kids couldn't get enough of this soup but wouldn't eat spinach any other way.

2 tablespoons salad oil
¾ cup chopped onion
1 large clove garlic crushed
6 cups water
6 chicken bouillon cubes
8 ounces fine egg noodles
1 teaspoon salt
6 cups milk
2 packages frozen chopped spinach
8 ounces shredded cheddar cheese (cooked and drained)
8 ounces shredded Swiss cheese
Paprika
Packaged croutons

In a large saucepan, heat the oil. Add the onion and garlic. Sauté over medium heat, stirring occasionally until the onion is tender—about 5 minutes. Add water and bouillon cubes. Heat to a rapid boil, stirring occasionally to dissolve the cubes. Add the noodles; salt so that the water continues to boil. Cook uncovered, stirring occasionally until the noodles are tender—about 6 minutes. Stir in the milk, spinach, cheese. Do not boil, but heat until all heated through. Sprinkle with paprika and add croutons at the table.

Serves 8 or 2 kids 4 times.

This is a beautiful first course for Christmas, too, with the green of the spinach and the red of the paprika.

Anne Underwood Grant mysteries include *Multiple Listing, Smoke Screen,* and *Cuttings.*

Green Chile Stew

CONNIE SHELTON

*H*ere's one of my favorite recipes (because it's easy to make), which my husband loves (he's crazy about chile) and I frequently serve to guests (it gives them an authentic taste of New Mexico). I think every New Mexican makes some version of Green Chile Stew, and each version is different, so you could probably do an entire cookbook of green chile stew recipes and manage to include no duplicates! Here's my version:

1 to 1 ½ pounds pork tenderloin, cut in ½-inch cubes
2 cans stewed tomatoes, crushed
1 small can mild whole green chiles (4 to 5 chile pods),
    cut into stew-size chunks
Hot green chile to your taste (I use about a tablespoon;
    a little bit can really heat this up)
1 medium onion, cut into stew-size chunks
2 to 3 cloves garlic, minced
8 to 10 cups beef bouillon
Salt and black pepper to taste
2 medium potatoes, peeled and cut into ½-inch cubes

Place all ingredients except the potatoes into a large stew pot or kettle. Bring to a boil, then cover, reduce heat, and simmer for 2 to 3 hours. (The beauty of this recipe is that you can start dinner in the early afternoon, then forget about it while you read or write!) About 30 to 45 minutes before you plan to serve, peel and cut the potatoes and add them to the stew (unless you like your potatoes mushy; in that case put them in earlier). Serve with corn bread, warm flour tortillas, or your other favorite bread. *Tip:* This is even better re-warmed the next day!

Connie Shelton is the author of the Charlie Parker mystery series, which includes *Small Towns Can Be Murder*, *Partnerships Can Kill*, and *Vacations Can Be Murder.*

Gazpacho to Kill For

JIM WEIKART

Since gazpacho is served up first, it's always a big hit because your guests are hungry. And since the tomatoes get riper and riper as summer goes on, your victims continue to think that you've improved on the recipe. Also, it's the easiest thing in the world to make. I impress the guests by letting them watch me do it.

Pick the tomatoes from a field under a full moon at midnight. Cop the cucumbers from a roadside veggie stand. Take the green pepper from a neighbor's home garden on the sly. Slice open a bag of onions at the supermarket and steal just one.

> 4 cups very ripe tomatoes, peeled and diced (4 to 6 good-size tomatoes)
> 1 cup chopped cucumbers (1 large cucumber)
> ½ cup chopped green pepper (½ large green pepper)
> ½ small onion, chopped
> ¾ teaspoon salt
> ½ teaspoon fresh ground black pepper
> ⅓ cup olive oil
> ¼ cup balsamic vinegar

Chop all the vegetables into a blender. I peel the tomatoes if the skin falls off, but otherwise leave it on. I do peel the cucumbers, unless I can guarantee they are fresh and unwaxed. Put in the salt and pepper. Being a little heavy with the pepper seems to work wonders with the flavors. Add the oil and vinegar. Blend and presto! A fresh and delicious cold soup. The closer to the time of eating it's made, the better it is.

Jim Weikart has written *Casualty Loss* and *Harry's Last Tax Cut*, as well as short stories for *Mystery Monthly* and *Ellery Queen Mystery Magazine*.

Meme's Taco Soup

PATSY WARD BURK

*I*n *The Knife Stuck Four*, Lieutenant Craig Isley of the Houston Police Department enjoys cooking, but doesn't have much time to devote to the hobby. One-dish meals, foods that will feed a crowd, or recipes that can be frozen are almost mandatory. Taco Soup qualifies as all three. I'll bet Lt. Isley would invite Carly St. Claire to join him for this favorite.

    1 pound ground meat (the less fat content the better, of course)
    1 onion, chopped
    1 green bell pepper, chopped
    1 32-ounce can (or 3 12-ounce)* Italian-style tomatoes
    2 cans pinto beans with juice
    1 can whole kernel corn with juice
    1 can hominy with juice
    1 8-ounce (or next larger size)* can tomato paste
    1 package taco seasoning mix
    1 small package (same size as taco mix) Hidden Valley Ranch dry dressing mix
    3 cups water (or more)*
    1 can chicken broth
    Salt and pepper to taste

Start with a big soup pot!!!

Brown meat with chopped onions and green bell pepper. Drain the fat. Chop the tomatoes into bite-size bits. Add the tomatoes and remaining ingredients to the mixture. Bring to a boil. Reduce heat and simmer for 1 hour, or 2—if the kids are late.

Keeps well in the fridge or freezes well if you can make it last long enough to freeze.

Patsy Ward Burk is the author of *The Knife Struck Four*.

* You know how grandmothers are—it's a pinch of this and a smidgen of that. Seriously, can sizes vary throughout the country, so don't worry about it if they don't have the exact size.

Betty Trenka's Bean Soup
JOYCE CHRISTMAS

One characteristic of retired office manager Betty Trenka is her marked lack of domesticity. She doesn't do crafts, she doesn't knit, she doesn't garden much, and she certainly doesn't cook. However, she does have one special recipe, thanks to her Czech mother. She makes bean soup with dropped noodles, a traditional family dish.

A big pot of bean soup is perfect for a cold Connecticut day, and it lasts a good long time, so Betty doesn't have to cook again for days.

> 1 pound (or more for a bigger pot of soup) dried white beans, Great Northern, for example, or for a quicker fix, 3 cans of white beans or a mixture of white, red and pink canned beans, drained and rinsed
> 2 tablespoons vegetable oil
> 1 medium onion, chopped
> 6 to 8 cups of chicken broth, heated
> 1 carrot, sliced
> A leftover ham bone, sliced kielbasa, or even sliced hot dogs (optional)
> Seasoning: salt, pepper, Italian seasoning, whatever

Noodles:

> 2 cups of flour
> 3 or 4 eggs
> ½ teaspoon salt

If using dried beans, rinse and put in a large soup pot with cold water about 2 inches higher than the beans. Bring to a boil for 2 or 3 minutes, cover, and remove from heat. Let stand for an hour, drain, rinse and return to the pot. In a small frying pan, sauté the onion in the oil until soft.

Add the hot chicken broth (enough to cover the beans), sautéed onions, and sliced carrot. If you have a ham bone, add that too. Cook over medium heat until the beans are soft. *Do not add any salt until beans are soft*, or else they will *never* get soft.

When the beans are done (an hour, more or less, depending on the type of beans), season to taste. If you are using canned beans, they need only to be heated with the other ingredients.

When the soup is hot, remove the ham bone and cut off any bits of meat, returning them to the pot. If you don't have a ham bone, you can use sliced kielbasa, a piece of ham cut in cubes, or even hot dogs. You don't really need any of them!

Make the noodle dough by adding the eggs to the flour and ½ teaspoon of salt. A little onion or garlic powder adds flavor. Mix thoroughly to the "consistency of library paste," as Betty's mother used to say. If the dough is too dry, add another egg and flour if needed or a very little bit of water.

When the beans are cooked, keep them bubbling, and drop bits of the dough into the boiling soup with a fork or small spoon. Bigger bits make bigger noodles, but traditionally they should be quite small. They are cooked when they rise to the top (a matter of a few minutes, but longer won't hurt them). The best test is to sample one.

This is what is called "a hearty meal."

Books in the Betty Trenka series by Joyce Christmas include *This Business is Murder, Death at Face Value* and *Downsized to Death.*

> *"I call it strange stew, said Janey, "because I put in everything strange I find left over in the icebox."*
>
> *The oldest daughter liked the pineapples, the youngest liked the mushrooms and the middle daughter thought the pickles added a nice touch.*
>
> *"You put in the cat food, ma?"*
>
> *"No, no cat food."*
>
> —Stephen Dobyns, *Saratoga Haunting*

Last Will and Testament Chowder

(*Warning:* This recipe is absolutely deadly for those on a low cholesterol diet.)

DORIAN YEAGER

𝒯his is one of my late father's (a part-time lobster fisherman) recipes, and though dangerous, it has never actually killed anyone. Frank Will's lobster stew is a running joke in my New
England-based Elizabeth Will mysteries. Elizabeth's father cooks up a honking batch whenever he's stressed out—which is most of the time, being Elizabeth's father, and all.

    1 stick (¼ pound) butter
    1 medium onion, chopped fine
    4 large potatoes, diced medium
    Choice of seafood (2 to 3 lobsters, boiled, bodies snapped apart, or 1 pound
        cleaned shrimp, or 2 big fistfuls raw oysters or clams or mussels)*
    2 quarts half-and-half
    Seasoned salt and pepper, to taste
    3 tablespoons fresh chives

Melt the butter in a Dutch oven. Add finely chopped onion and potatoes, and simmer until
the onions are translucent but not browned.

If making lobster stew, toss in the bodies with both quarts of half-and-half. Bring to a boil.
Turn off the heat and let set several hours (overnight is best for those who are not squeamish.)
Remove the bodies.

For all other variations, add the half-and-half along with your choice of seafood, and bring
the mixture to a boil. Turn off the heat and let set 2 to 3 hours minimum. The more the potatoes cook down, the thicker the chowder will be. Bring back to a boil and serve, garnished
with fresh chives—or my preference, fresh chopped garlic chives—and a splash of seasoned
salt for floating color. Oyster crackers are *de rigeur*, but hardly necessary if you have a crusty
loaf of bread.

Recommended for freezing in good-quality zipper-closure plastic bags in small servings.

Serves 6 people, or 2 commercial fisherman.

*Substitute 1 or 2 cans of creamed corn in place of seafood for a *wicked good* corn chowder.

Dorian Yeager is the author of two mystery series. Her books include *Cancel-
lation by Death* featuring Victoria Bowering and *Murder Will Out* featuring
Elizabeth Will.

Chef d'Oeuvre

*E*nglish mystery master Nicolas Freeling, creator of both Dutch police-man Piet van der Valk and Parisian Police Judiciaire officer Henri Castang, began his adult life as a professional cook, an apprenticeship he chronicles to hilarious effect in his culinary memoir *The Kitchen Book*. English-born, Freeling spent part of his childhood in Le Croisic on the Loire estuary and, later, in Saint Malo. His father died when he was twelve, leaving the impressionable boy several "cookery" books, which Nicholas read at night the way other adolescents read comic books or dime novels.

When he came out of the army, it seemed only natural to Freeling that he pursue a life in the kitchen. Starting in the larder of a Paris hotel, he later went to work at the Hotel Atlantic in Belleplage, a Victorian relic in a second-rate resort town. In his spirited literary remembrances, he intro-duces readers to a motley, international collection of chefs and kitchen help more colorful than any fiction writer could imagine. He recounts the way things were done in those classic French kitchens and shares some of his own hard-earned knowledge about the expert handling of food. In a second book, *The Cook Book*, Freeling spurns traditional recipes with his own free-wheeling narrative on how to make some of his own favorites.

In his inimitable style, Freeling ruminates on the essential tools of both his chosen professions: *My right hand, throughout my life the weaker, strengthens slowly since I have earned my living from writing and comes to bal-ance the left which has lost the special skills and sensitivity of a cook, the rapidity and dexterity (or right-handed skill) it once had. It is now truly the sinister hand, humble servant of the other—I use it to type with. The right hand had to be apprenticed like the left, and learned that writing like cooking is a trade painfully acquired.* Fittingly, Freeling started his first mystery novel, *Love in Amsterdam*, while serving a three-week jail sentence for stealing food. The food lover's loss was most assuredly the mystery lover's gain.

Lansdale Chili

JOE R. LANSDALE

This recipe was used as part of a promotion for my book *Bad Chili*. Also, a short story, "Death by Chili" was published with it, and readers who attended the bookstore festivities had to guess the outcome.

It's a simple fact that the best chili and barbecue in the world comes from Texas. It's not a subject for discussion.

First, you cook a lot of hamburger meat. I'm not sure how much is a lot, but you know, a lot. Anyway, you brown it, drain off the grease, and put it in a pot. Now cut some steak into strips and brown it; cut this up in chunks and put it in the pot.

Add a couple of cups of water and 6 to 12 ounces of tomato paste. Put in 2 teaspoons of sugar, 4 teaspoons of chili powder, and 10 cut-up juicy jalapeño peppers. Stir and add more water; be your own judge, but don't make it too watery.

Now, a dash of cayenne pepper, a dash of Tabasco sauce, a teaspoon of garlic powder or some real chunks of garlic, add 1 tablespoon of olive oil—that's so it won't all clog up like a brick inside you.

Cut up 2 to 3 medium ripe tomatoes and toss this into the mix. Slice up a small onion and add it. Add ½ teaspoon of oregano, 1 or 2 tablespoons of black pepper, and ½ cup of ketchup.

Let this simmer for a damn long time, adding water when needed, but don't add too much. Keep it thick. If it looks a little watery, then add more ingredients. It's better at this point to add a cat or a parakeet than it is to add too much water.

After a few hours take a Pepcid and have chili. If it doesn't taste quite right, you probably followed the recipe too closely or didn't take enough Pepcid. Throw it back into the pot, add some more of everything but water, and try again. (If your chili comes out of the pan in wads, then maybe you do need to add some water!)

Note: We had success using the following quantities:

> 3 ½ pounds hamburger
> 2 ½ pounds steak
> 3 cups water

We used a medium-high heat once the water, etc., was added to the pot. Before letting the mix simmer we added another ½ cup of water, turned the heat to medium, and simmered for about 45 minutes.

If making this on a blistering hot day as we did, we suggest a cool shower (or a margarita or two) while the chili simmers!

Serves 15 as a main course.

Joe R. Lansdale's suspense novels include *Mucho Mojo*, *Cold in July*, and *Savage Season*.

Cincinnati Chili

CATHIE JOHN

Kate Cavanaugh, one of Cincinnati's favorite gourmet caterers, is also the heir to the Crown Chili fortune. In her first escapade, Kate finds herself embroiled in the mysterious death of her friend Preston Schneider, the local Restaurant Critic from Hell. Preston was well known for his sarcastic remarks and biting reviews. One of his most famous comments is: *"The culinary scene in Cincinnati consists of one astronomically expensive five star restaurant and a couple hundred chili parlors."* There are hundreds of versions of the recipe for Cincinnati Chili, but they're basically all the same. However, some are guarded secrets, with their spice mixture being put together behind closed doors. Enclosed is Kate's favorite version, which also happens to be her family's recipe, having been handed down through the generations from Kate's great-great-grandpa to her father—"The Chili Kings", as Kate affectionately calls them.

2 pounds lean ground beef
2 onions, chopped
4 cloves garlic, minced
16-ounce can tomato sauce
2 tablespoons vinegar
2 teaspoons Worcestershire sauce
½ teaspoon ground allspice

½ teaspoon ground cloves
2 teaspoons cinnamon
1 teaspoon cumin
½ teaspoon cayenne pepper
2 tablespoons chili powder
½ ounce unsweetened chocolate, grated

Crumble raw ground beef into one quart of boiling water. This looks disgusting, but hang in there, it'll eventually cook down into a more appetizing-looking concoction. **Do not brown the ground beef first.** Stir in rest of the ingredients, return to a boil, then reduce heat and simmer, uncovered, for 2 to 2 ½ hours. Stir occasionally as it cooks.

To serve: For a 2-way: Spaghetti topped with chili
For a 3-way: Spaghetti topped with chili and lots of shredded, mild cheddar cheese.
For a 4-way: Spaghetti topped with chili, mild cheddar cheese, and chopped onion.
For a 5-way: Same as 4-way but top each serving with cooked red kidney beans.

Whatever way you have it, it should be served with bowls of oyster crackers and, for those who want it hotter, red pepper sauce.

To know if your Cincinnati Chili is made correctly, your lips should tingle when you eat it.

(Optional: Refrigerate cooked chili overnight for better flavor.)

A Coney is a hot dog on a bun, topped with chili, onions, and shredded cheddar cheese.

Cathie John's Kate Cavanaugh mysteries include *Beat a Rotten Egg to the Punch* and *Add One Dead Critic*.

RESSED TO KILL

Warm Pear and Stilton Salad

PETER ROBINSON

_D_etective Chief Inspector Alan Banks is a man who loves justice and good food. Although not much of a cook himself, even he would be able to manage this!

> Half as many pears as there are diners
> Chunk of Stilton cheese
> Mixed green salad
> Vinaigrette dressing
> Chopped walnuts

Halve the pears, but don't peel them. Scoop out the center of each half pear and add a generous amount of Stilton. (You can also add a pinch of nutmeg or cinnamon if you wish). Stick the halves back together and wrap them in foil. If the weather's fine, you can barbecue the pears on medium heat for 5 minutes or so, until the outer surface feels a little soft to the touch. If it's raining, you can use a 350-degree oven for 5 or 10 minutes—again, until the outside gives a little to the touch. (You don't want them to be _too_ soft.)

Heat a skillet and carefully toast the chopped walnuts, taking care they don't burn.

Assemble the salad and dressing, serve, then place half a pear on top of each portion. Sprinkle with the toasted chopped walnuts.

This makes a great appetizer, but if you wish, you could cut the rabbit food and enjoy it as a dessert—preferably with a nice glass of port or some chilled sauternes!

Bon appétit!

Peter Robinson's non-cooking Inspector Banks appears in _Wednesday's Child_, _Final Account_ and _In a Dry Season_.

Insalata Caprese

WILLIAM MURRAY

Horseplayers like Shifty Lou Anderson don't eat much, especially at the track. But here's a salad—it's the best lunch you can buy, a perfect summer dish.

> The best, meaning the freshest, mozzarella *di bufala* you can buy
> Vine-grown tomatoes
> Fresh basil leaves
> Sea salt
> Olive oil

Slice the mozzarella and tomatoes, then stack them together, alternating slices. Tear up some fresh basil leaves and sprinkle over the tomatoes and cheese. Add sea salt and the best olive oil you can buy.

Add fresh crusty bread to mop up the remnants.

William Murray's mysteries, set at the racetrack and featuring Shifty Lou Anderson include *Tip On A Dead Crab* and *We're Off to See the Killer.*

Cold Noodle Salad with Spicy Peanut Sauce

TRISS STEIN

My heroine, Kay Engels, is a busy reporter who doesn't have the time or desire to cook, but she likes good food, and restaurant meals seem to creep into all my writing about her. The first and third books take place in upstate New York farm country, where she enjoys the modest local restaurants serving homemade pies, fresh fish, great cheddar cheese, and old-fashioned Italian cooking. In *Digging Up Death*, she is back home in New York City, where she loves the endless variety of cuisines New York offers, including spicy Asian cooking. She would enjoy this dish, if someone else did the cooking.

Note to those who do cook: This is probably not very authentic, but it is infinitely adaptable; a great way to use up leftovers. And the spicy flavors combine with the chilled temperature to make it especially appealing in hot, humid, appetite-killing weather. It's delicious at room temperature, too.

Peanut Sauce:

½ cup creamy peanut butter
¼ cup warm water
¼ cup chopped green onion
2 clovers garlic, crushed
¼ cup soy sauce

¼ cup peanut oil
2 tablespoons wine vinegar
4 tablespoons sugar
1 teaspoon salt
½ teaspoon cayenne pepper

Any 2 of the following, or any crunchy vegetable available:

4 cups fresh bean sprouts
2 cups shredded Chinese cabbage
  or iceberg lettuce
1 cup slivered radishes
1 cup carrots, sliced thinly, crosswise
1 cup slivered green peppers

1 package fine egg noodles, or leftover
  other noodles or thin spaghetti,
2 teaspoons peanut oil
2 cups (½ pound) roast pork or roast beef
  or cooked steak, veal, or chicken (this is
  optional—it's a good vegetarian dish, too)

In a small bowl, combine peanut butter and water until smooth. Add the remaining sauce ingredients. Stir until well mixed; chill at least 4 hours or overnight.

Cook the egg noodles according to package directions. Drain; rinse under cold water; drain again. Place in a bowl, toss with 2 teaspoons of oil, cover, and refrigerate. If using leftover noodles, just toss with oil and use.

To serve, put the noodles in individual bowls or salad plates. Arrange the vegetables and meat attractively on a platter. Let everyone serve themselves, and pass the sauce. (Or, of course, you can mix everything together in a big bowl, keep in the refrigerator and eat over a few a days!)

Triss Stein is the author of *Digging Up Death* and *Murder at the Class Reunion*.

Night-in-the-Cooler Eggplant Salad
NATHAN WALPOW

I often bring this dish when invited to a potluck or similar event. So does Joe Portugal, the cactus-collecting sleuth in my series of botanical mysteries. It's always a big hit at the annual cactus-and -succulent club picnic, and I figured if cactus folks in the real world like it, the ones in Joe's fictional one would too. It's one of only three dishes Joe knows how to make by heart.

Though Joe never remembers to make it the night before, I always do, because it tastes better after sitting in the refrigerator overnight. Hence the name.

    2 medium eggplants
    4 to 6 Roma or 2 to 3 large tomatoes
    3 scallions
    Juice of 1 ½ lemons
    ¾ teaspoon ground cumin
    ½ teaspoon ground coriander
    ½ teaspoon ground turmeric
    ¼ teaspoon ground ginger
    ¼ teaspoon ground red pepper
    ⅛ teaspoon ground cinnamon
    black pepper

Prick the eggplants with a fork. Place on a cookie sheet and bake in 350-degree oven for 45 minutes to 1 hour, until very well done. Let cool, then spoon the flesh into mixing bowl, discarding skin. Finely chop the tomatoes and scallions; mix with eggplant. Add the juice of 1 lemon. Combine the spices and blend into the eggplant mixture. Add black pepper and additional lemon juice to taste. Refrigerate.

Serve with triangles of pita bread.

Nathan Walpow's *The Cactus Club Killings* introduces Joe Portugal, a cactus-collecting TV-commercial actor.

Now you know, I truly hesitated over whether or not to add anise. Not everyone cares for it, but it's typically Italian. Oh, not with an oil-and-vinegar dressing perhaps, but plain oil and vinegar are so unadventurous, and cooking should always be an adventure, don't you agree?

—Margaret Maron, *One Coffee With*

Asparagus and Pepper Salad

SKYE ALEXANDER

*W*hen I was a girl I used to pick wild asparagus with my mother in the mountains of western North Carolina, where my book *Hidden Agenda* takes place. This colorful salad is a refreshing first course during hot weather—like the heat wave that adds fuel to the fury in *Hidden Agenda.*

> 1 pound fresh asparagus
> 1 medium red pepper
> 1 medium yellow pepper
> ⅛ cup red wine vinegar
> 1 tablespoon olive oil
> ¼ cup chopped fresh arugula
> 2 tablespoons chopped fresh basil
> 1 tablespoon salted sunflower seeds

Cut the tough bottoms off the asparagus spears. Cut the peppers into thin strips (remove seeds and stems). Steam together until tender but not mushy. Allow to cool. Blend the vinegar, oil, basil, and arugula, then pour over the vegetables and toss. Sprinkle with sunflower seeds and chill well.

Serves 4 as a side dish or 2 as a healthy, light meal.

Skye Alexander is the author of *Hidden Agenda* in the Magical Mystery series.

The Salad Dressing
of Colonel Cray

$\mathcal{G}$.K. Chesterton's short story "The Salad of Colonel Cray" from *The Wisdom of Father Brown* finds the sagacious priest challenged by a peculiar mystery involving an alleged curse bestowed on the hapless Colonel Cray while he was stationed in India. Since the curse, more than one attempt has been made on poor Cray's life. Now, back in England, he is staying with a fellow Anglo-Indian officer when a burglar steals the household silver, including a salad cruet-stand.

A gunshot and a sneeze are just two of the clues that lead Father Brown to his nick-of-time solution. And the cruet-stand, retrieved from the dustbin, proves a timely discovery when one of the ingredients in the vinaigrette dressing provides an urgent emetic for Colonel Cray, who has been poisoned.

Here's a classic vinaigrette as the versatile Father Brown might have mixed it that fateful day at lunch with Colonel Cray.

3 tablespoons white wine vinegar
¼ teaspoon dry mustard, or 1 teaspoon prepared Dijon mustard
Salt and fresh-ground black pepper to taste
½ cup olive oil

Mix together vinegar, mustard, salt and pepper. Add the oil gradually, beating with a whisk. Serve on fresh greens.

My Mother's La Venida Caesar Salad

JOHN GILSTRAP

Given a choice, I believe that my mother would have lived on a diet of lobster tails and salads. She was famous within the family for suddenly discovering a lobster tail in the back of the freezer just when the rest of us had sat down to our pork chops or grilled cheese sandwiches. "Since you're already eating…"

So I suppose the truest tribute to Mom would have been to provide a lobster recipe, but I figured that *Put frozen lobster tail under broiler until done* would run a little short for our purposes here. Besides, I'm allergic to lobster.

Truth be told, Mom wasn't much of a cook. I think she got bored with all the preparation. There was, however, at least one from-scratch dish that the entire extended family eagerly awaited and that became a dinnertime staple whenever guests came to the house: Her Caesar salad.

But first, the story behind the story.

Nothing about Mom's tastes in food was ordinary. As a child, when all the other kids would sneak candy into the movie theater for the Saturday matinee, she would stop by the local deli and buy a kosher dill pickle as her treat. I try to imagine what it must have been like watching some of the classic movies—*Gone With The Wind*, *Casablanca*, *The Wizard of Oz*—with the odor of garlicky pickle juice hanging like a cloud over the seats. Kinda makes my eyes water.

Anyway, it should be no surprise that her pregnancy cravings were unusual as well. Family legend has it that when she was pregnant with my older brother, she craved only one thing: The Caesar salad from the La Venida Restaurant in Coronado, CA. My dad was in the Navy at the time, and day or night, rain or shine, he made countless runs to the beloved eatery to pick up one of those delicacies for his bride.

The cravings and deliveries all ran their course four years before I was born, yet for my entire life, I accepted as fact that the best salad in the universe was the mystical "Lava Needa"—or was it the more exotic "Lav Anita?"—salad. I never questioned it. It was one of those things I just knew to be true because my mother told me so. Like, "No, there's nothing wrong with Uncle Joe, people just act that way sometimes."

I was grown and married before I had my first opportunity to visit Coronado (where, I'll have you know, my grandfather helped carve the grand staircase in the famed Hotel Del Coronado), and on our very first night there, my wife and I sought out the La Venida restaurant, whose owner swore that he still remembered my parents after thirty-odd years. We ordered the salad, of course, and guess what? My mother's famed Caesar salad was, in fact, made from the same recipe as the "Lava Needa!" Who'd have guessed?

I'm told by my brother, who recently returned from a trip to southern California, that La Venida is no longer in business. A bit of family history is gone. But truth be told, having sampled them both, I think Mom's salad was better.

It goes wonderfully with lobster tails.

    1 clove garlic
    ¼ cup vegetable oil (½ cup for larger servings)
    1 egg
    ¼ cup lemon juice
    1 drop Worcestershire sauce
    Salt and pepper
    Parmesan cheese, grated
    Romaine lettuce
    Seasoned croutons

Crush the garlic clove and let sit in oil for at least 1 hour (the longer the better). In a separate bowl, mix the egg, lemon juice, Worcestershire sauce, salt and pepper. While stirring the mixture gently, add Parmesan cheese until thick. When the lettuce is torn, remove the garlic from the oil and pour the oil over the lettuce. Toss thoroughly. Add the Parmesan cheese mixture and toss again. Add croutons and serve immediately.

John Gilstrap is the author of *Nathan's Run* and *At All Costs*.

Belgian Endive Salad

PETER ABRESCH

This is taken from an Elderhostel at the Chef's Culinary College of Baltimore. Beautiful chef Nina Achilles tasted this Belgian Endive Salad and expired on the spot. Croaked. The thing that baffled amateur sleuths, Jim Dandy, and his lady friend, Dodee Swisher, is that Neill Cockburn tossed the salad in full view of the cooking class, and tasted it, twice, just seconds before Chef Achilles, with no ill effects. Aside from a few delicious murders, Elderhostelers Jim Dandy and Dodee Swisher had a great time at the Culinary College in Baltimore.

> 6 Belgian endive, cut into ¼-thick slices
> ½ cup walnuts, broken
> 2 apples, sliced
> 2 tablespoons lemon juice
> 6 tablespoons olive oil
> Salt to taste

Trim and slice endive; place in colander and rinse. Drain well. Put the endive in a salad bowl and sprinkle with the walnuts. Toss the apples in lemon juice in a separate bowl. Add the apple mixture to endive. Sprinkle with olive oil. Toss. Season with salt. Serve.

Unless, maybe, you'd like to add a pinch of arsenic?

Peter Abresch's James P. Dandy Elderhostel mysteries include *Bloody Bonsai* and *Killing Thyme*.

KNEADLESS VIOLENCE

Sharon McCone's Garlic Bread

MARCIA MULLER

*P*rivate investigator Sharon McCone, like her creator, loves Italian food. She makes a terrific lasagna and is always promising to cook up a batch for her friends. So far as I know, however, no one has ever eaten her lasagna; she keeps getting called away on a case and having to store it in her freezer. Upon occasion, though, she has served her special garlic bread, and the recipe for it follows:

> 1 stick butter
> 8 to 12 cloves garlic (more if you like garlic), finely minced
> 1 loaf extra-sour sourdough bread, split lengthwise
> 2 cups shredded Parmesan cheese (or more of that too)
> Paprika

Melt the butter, and simmer the garlic in it for about 3 minutes. Pour evenly onto the bread. Top with shredded cheese, sprinkle with paprika. Bake in a 350-degree oven for about 10 minutes, then broil till the cheese browns. Serve quickly, in case *you* get called away on an investigation!

Just a few of Marcia Muller's Sharon McCone mysteries are *While Other People Sleep*, *Trophies and Dead Things*, and *Leave a Message for Willie*.

Crusty Fat-Free Bread

GILLIAN ROBERTS

You can make this while writing—the punching, kneading and slashing of the loaves can be very therapeutic…and the end result is dangerously good.

> 1 package active dry yeast
> 1 tablespoon each salt and sugar
> Approximately 5 cups all-purpose flour
> Cornmeal

Dissolve the yeast in 2 cups of lukewarm water. Add the salt and sugar and mix well. With a wooden spoon, beat in enough flour, 1 cup at a time, to form a smooth ball that clears side of bowl. Knead and set to rise, covered, for 1 ½ hours, or until doubled. With your hands, stir down, turn onto a floured board, knead a few turns, then cut in half. Shape each half into a loaf about 12 inches long. Put on a baking sheet well-sprinkled with cornmeal. Let rise 5 minutes, then slash the tops in 4 places with a sharp knife. Brush with water and put into a cold oven that has a pan of boiling water on its bottom rack. Turn the oven to 400 degrees and bake 40 minutes, or until crusty and browned. Best served hot.

Gillian Roberts' series about high-school English teacher Amanda Pepper includes *Caught Dead in Philadelphia*, and *Philly Stakes*. Her new series about San Francisco Bay Area investigator Emma Howe debuted with *Time and Trouble*.

Fred Lundquist's Sourdough Oatmeal Bread
SARA HOSKINSON FROMMER

*J*oan Spencer, my viola-playing sleuth, is a hurry-up cook not inclined to anything fancy. Me, too.

Her friend Detective Lieutenant Fred Lundquist, on the other hand, is an accomplished baker who made bread for an Oliver, Indiana, caterer in *Murder in C Major*, until she—well, never mind what she did. Here's a passage where he's just starting with a sourdough recipe (not oatmeal).

> *Lundquist trudged upstairs to his sterile rooms, remembering only after releasing his tired feet from their leather prisons that he had promised Catherine sourdough bread for a large party she was catering Saturday night. He retrieved the starter from its covered dish at the back of the refrigerator, divided it into two bowls, and added flour, water, and a spoonful of sugar to activate the culture. Gluten flour in one and rye in the other. If she wanted variety, he'd give it to her. Covering the lumpy messes, he cleared his mind. Five minutes later, he slept.*

Fred's bread, which I've been making for many years, is a family favorite. It makes wonderful toast, too, although when it's fresh you can hardly think of toasting it.

Bread baking is a natural for a mystery writer. Unlike rolling out pie dough, which requires a light, happy touch, you can knead bread successfully when you're furious. Leaning into a big mound of bread dough, I plot killing all kinds of people.

If you've never baked bread, you probably want to try something else first. This one is sticky, but it's so good and moist.

You need about ¼ cup of sourdough starter. Ask a friend—Fred never buys yeast, but he never forgets to save his starter for next time. It lasts months. He doesn't keep "feeding" it, and it doesn't grow into a refrigerator monster.

The night before you bake:

> 1 tablespoon sugar
> 4 cups all-purpose or bread flour
> 4 ½ cups warm water

Mix the starter with the above ingredients. Let it stand overnight, covered, in a large non-metal bowl.

The next day (it's okay if you don't get to it first thing):

Save some starter for next time. Just ¼ cup is plenty. Put it in a 1-cup glass jar or plastic bowl with a lid, and stick it on a back shelf in the refrigerator. Ignore it.

> ½ cup sugar
> ⅔ cup nonfat dry milk
> ¼ cup oil
> 1 ½ teaspoons salt
> 4 cups uncooked quick oats
> 4 cups warm water (about 115 degrees, not too hot for yeast)
> 8 to 9 cups all-purpose or bread flour

To the rest of the sourdough in the bowl, which should be stretchy and have some bubbles, add the sugar and stir in gently with a non-metal spoon. Then add the milk, oil, salt, quick oats, and water. Stir gently again. Last, gradually add the flour. When you can't stir any more into the dough, turn it out onto a floured board or table. This is the really sticky part! Mix the rest in with your hands, and knead until the dough is elastic and not too sticky, adding flour as needed. Resist the temptation to add so much that it's not sticky at all. You want moist bread.

Oil the inside of a non-metal bowl and let the bread rise, covered with a damp towel, until doubled. Even on a hot day it will take 2 or 3 hours for the first rising. On a cold day, it will take longer. If you don't have a big enough bowl, use two. (Consider kneading raisins into one bowl of dough.) When it has doubled, punch the dough down and divide it to shape 4 loaves. Place in greased bread pans. (Or use some for rolls. Place on a greased cookie sheet or pizza pan. Don't make them small; they're very crusty.)

Let the loaves rise in the pans to within an inch of the top of the pan. Bake at 450 degrees for 10 minutes, and then lower to 350 degrees and bake for 40 to 50 minutes, until brown on top and easy to remove. (For rolls: bake 10 minutes at 450 degrees and then lower to 350 degrees and bake 20 minutes.)

Freeze extra bread in plastic bags to keep it fresh.

Fred Lundquist and Joan Spencer appear in Sara Hoskinson Frommer's *Murder in C Major, Buried in Quilts,* and *Murder & Sullivan.*

Not So "Stout" Blueberry Muffins

"I descended a flight to Wolfe's room, tapped on the door, and entered. He was in bed, propped up against three pillows, just ready to attack the provender on the breakfast table which straddled his mountainous ridge under the black silk coverlet. There was orange juice, eggs au berre noir, *two slices of broiled Georgia ham, hashed brown potatoes, hot blueberry muffins, and a pot of steaming cocoa."*

—Rex Stout, *Over My Dead Body*

Perhaps Nero Wolfe wouldn't have been quite as "mountainous" had he substituted these low-fat, yet delicious blueberry muffins in his prodigious breakfast menu.

2 cups all-purpose flour
½ cup sugar
3 teaspoons baking powder
½ teaspoon salt
¾ cup low-fat (or skim) milk
3 tablespoons oil
1 egg, beaten
1 ½ cup fresh blueberries (if using frozen, do not thaw)

Heat the oven to 400 degrees. Grease the muffin tins with low-fat coating spray (or line tins with paper baking cups).

In a medium bowl, combine the flour, sugar, baking powder and salt; mix well with a fork. In a separate bowl, combine the milk, oil, and beaten egg; blend well. Add the wet ingredients to the flour mixture and stir until the dry ingredients are moist. Do not over stir. Gently stir in the blueberries.

Divide the batter evenly among the muffin cups. Bake for 18 to 23 minutes or until light golden brown. Cool for 1 minute before removing from pan. Best when served warm, but still tasty the next day (if Wolfe hasn't devoured them all).

Makes 12 standard-size or 8 large muffins.

QUICK AND PAINLESS

The Kinsey Millhone Famous Peanut Butter and Pickle Sandwich

SUE GRAFTON

I get letters from readers who are completely aghast at the notion of eating such a concoction, but others actually try it (with relatives standing by to dial 911) and confess it's not half bad. Strangely yummy, they say. Some readers take a jauntier attitude and begin to try improvements, a course Kinsey and I are quick to discourage. The following is the actual, true, unadulterated recipe for the Kinsey Millhone Famous Peanut Butter and Pickle Sandwich.

> 2 slices of Health-Nut bread, or some whole-grain equivalent
> Gobs of Jif crunchy peanut butter (no substitutions, please)
> Vlasic sweet butter chips* (again, no substitutions or we can't be
>   responsible for the result)

Spread gobs of Jif crunchy peanut butter on 1 slice of Health-Nut bread. Place 6 or 7 Vlasic sweet butter chips on the peanut butter. Top with second slice of bread. Cut on the diagonal.

Serves 1.

*When we mentioned Vlasic sweet butter chips by name in a well-known food-related magazine, Vlasic sent me a *case* of sweet butter chips. Let's hope the Jif crunchy peanut butter people are just as generous in response to our *product loyalty*.

> Sue Grafton's Kinsey Millhone alphabet mysteries include *"A" is for Alibi* and *"N" is for Noose*.

Salami à la Chama River

TONY HILLERMAN

Remove a pack of cotto salami; a loaf of fresh-baked kosher rye bread; dill pickle; medium-size, full-ripe, morning-picked Celebrity tomato; 2 slice of iceberg lettuce; and a jar of mayonnaise from the ice chest in back of the Jeep.

Put a slice of rye on the chest lid, spread a thin layer of mayo on it with your fish knife. Apply 1 slice of salami. Cut 4 very thin slices of dill pickle. Place above salami. Place a layer of lettuce atop pickle slices. Cut 3 thin slices of tomato, and place atop lettuce. Place a second slice of salami on this. Top all with a second slice of rye.

Allow the above-mentioned ingredients to get acquainted while you seat yourself on a shaded boulder on the bank of the Brazos. Allow your feet to dangle in the current. Inhale several lungfuls (lungsful?) of cold, clean mountain air; consider the fly you will tie on to fool the big brook trout you spotted feeding in the ripples upstream.

Consume your Salami à la Chama River.

Tony Hillerman's series featuring Navajo tribal policemen Joe Leaphorn and Jim Chee includes *The First Eagle*, *A Thief of Time* and *Skinwalkers*.

The Great British Bacon Buttie

LIZA CODY

$\mathcal{M}$y two main characters, Anna Lee and Eva (Bucket Nut) Wylie, have almost nothing in common except that they spend even less time in the kitchen than I do. Anna might grill a chop or throw a salad together if she wasn't too pressed for time. Whereas Eva's culinary skills run more to opening a can of pork and beans and eating them straight from the can with a spoon. She might just heat them up if she's feeling particularly fastidious. But Anna and Eva do share a passion for a well-made bacon buttie, or sarnie.

The bacon sandwich is *not* a healthy eater's idea of dietary excellence, as it derives from a time when animal fat was thought to be good for you because it "kept out the cold." It was always a poor person's delicacy, as in, "I really fancy a bacon buttie, and if I had any bacon, I'd make one—if I had any bread."

Over here, in Britain, it's still a blue-collar favorite, and it's definitely *my* idea of comfort food—but then *I'm* not a Californian.

Take a cold, depressing day and as many thinly sliced rashers of smoked bacon as you think you can jam between two slices of bread. Fry the bacon in its own fat until it's crispy.

Drain and remove from the pan. Keep hot and dry on kitchen paper. Fry the bread in the bacon fat (on one side only) until both slices are evenly brown and crisp. Blot on kitchen paper.

The bacon goes between the crisp sides of the bread so that the sandwich is cool and squishy on the outside but hot and crunchy in the middle when you bite into it. Wash down with a mug of hot, strong tea. And—hey, presto—instant warmth and comfort plus all the excitement of risking a coronary.

Anna Lee, the fictional detective created by Liza Cody, appears in *Monkey Wrench*, *Dupe*, and *Bad Company*.

Charlie Plato's Killer Turkey Sandwich

MARGARET CHITTENDEN

I'm a fanatic on turkey sandwiches and am convinced there is a conspiracy afoot in the country to get rid of all real sliced turkey and fob off on us gelatinous, thin, deli turkey that doesn't even have a grain to it. Restaurants serve what they say is oven-roasted turkey sandwiches, or turkey-breast sandwiches, and waiters will swear up and down it's the real thing and it's not. We've reached the stage where waiters don't even remember what real turkey looks like. Now grocery stores are putting out packages of this impostor. I'm reduced to cooking whole turkeys at home just to make sandwiches. I've thought of taking Polaroid pictures of the turkey meat to show waiters. I can't seem to get anyone else excited about this dire situation, so I'm using Charlie Plato as my mouthpiece.

> *I perked up when I saw some real sliced turkey and sandwich makings. Not deli turkey made up of pressed bits taken from who knew what area of the turkey carcass, you understand, but the real, and increasingly rare, white and tender-looking breast meat. Beside the platter was a wooden serving board holding dense-looking whole-wheat bread that had sprouts sticking out of it. And there was a bowl of mesclun too that wonderful salad made of exotic leaves like arugula, mâche, red oak leaf, sorrel, frisée and radicchio. I had died and gone to heaven.*
> —from *Dead Beat and Deadly*

Start with 2 slices of 100 percent stone ground whole-wheat or multigrain bread. Spread 1 slice with gutless mayonnaise (no egg, low-fat.) Spread the other slice with a skinny scraping of Gorgonzola cheese. Fill with slices of real turkey breast, onion and crisp romaine.

Margaret Chittenden's turkey-loving sleuth Charlie Plato also appears in *Dying to Sing* and *Dead Men Don't Dance*.

Cowgirl's Quesadillas

SARAH ANDREWS

"Don't laugh—these are superior junk food. Em Hansen, my Wyoming-born geologist sleuth, has mastered the art of adapting Mexican classics to "northern" tastes. Em is not the nesting sort, and in fact has no permanent home, let alone a kitchen to call her own. But she can whip these wonders out over a hot plate or even in one of the unhygienic microwave ovens one finds in the trailers on an oil-drilling location.

Tortillas (wheat or corn, to taste)
Peanut butter, *or*
Cheese, sliced or grated to which add as desired:
Canned refried beans
Jalapeño peppers
Even a little cooked shredded chicken, if available
Lettuce to garnish, if you're feeling like a health fanatic.

If working over a burner, use a heavy skillet if available or simply apply tortilla directly to the burner and don't get distracted. Heat it up, taking care not to incinerate it. Apply (a) peanut butter or (b) cheese-bean-pepper-chicken combo, and heat carefully until the (a) peanut butter warms or (b) cheese melts. In case (b) add lettuce after removing from heat. Fold quesadilla in half and eat. If working with a microwave oven, add the ingredients directly to the tortilla and heat for about 45 seconds, then remove, add lettuce if (b), and enjoy.

Sarah Andrews is the author of the Em Hansen mysteries, which include *Tensleep*, *A Fall in Denver*, and *Mother Nature*.

We ordered our usual postmeeting dinners—a chili-burger for me and a plate of sliced tomatoes and cottage cheese for Lars. It was to this unvarying evening repast, cholesterol doom-sayers to the contrary, that Lars Jenssen attributed both his good health and his longevity.
     —J.A. Jance, *Payment in Kind*

Fred Taylor's Beans On Toast

NICHOLAS KILMER

"Fred jokes about food," apologizes the aesthete art collector Clayton Reed (who is also Fred's employer) to a fellow gourmet in *O Sacred Head*. Clayton, surprised in an ostentatious restaurant, is addressing what the menu bills as Coquilles St. Jacques, which Fred can see only as *"scallops accompanied by labor-intensive vegetables."* Fred refuses to join Clayton's dinner party, claiming that, in the spirit of the Italian Baroque, he has already enjoyed Banana St. Bartholomew: That is to say, a banana that has been prepared by flaying.

Fred presents himself, in his rather stubborn way, as a man who has *"a respect for materials. He liked his food to look like food, not like a hat or a boat or a day at the races." (Harmony in Flesh and Black)*. He itches if cooking and eating are confused with art or recreation. When surrounded by pretentious diners—for instance, at the Ritz dining room—Fred tends toward the obstreperous and occasionally delivers himself of recipes that, for all their respect for materials, would call for considerable time, skill, and financial outlay were you to undertake them—unless you already own a horse. Take, for example, a "favorite recipe" he cites (without giving the dish a name), which he suggests may have contributed to the ill-humor of the Mongol warrior during the time of Genghis Khan. *"It's simple. A slab of dried horseflesh is placed under the saddle at first light. The warrior spends his day riding, raping, and pillaging, never dismounting; in the evening he pulls out the slab, which has by this time softened and absorbed sufficient moisture as to be palatable."*

Knowing his rudimentary approach to culinary matters, Fred's lover, Molly Riley, becomes wary when he offers to throw a meal together for her little family. *"How about Spaghetti al Fred?"* Fred asks. *"If that means fried or broiled, maybe not,"* Molly says. *"The package suggests placing it in hot water,"* Fred persists. *"Try that way,"* Molly agrees. *"But first remove it from the box."* (*Man with a Squirrel*).

Supposing that any recipe that issues from Fred has come the hard way, we may not care to try everything he makes for himself when he learns that he is hungry. His Noodles with Uncanned Smoked Oysters (*Interior at Petworth*) may or may not be worth a try. With this caution—and with the assurance that the author has tried it and still puts it before you—here is Fred Taylor's Beans on Toast.

Find a saucepan, dump its contents, and wash it. Open a can of baked beans and put the beans into the saucepan to heat. Do the right thing with the empty can. Other people use this kitchen.

Make the toast. Put the toast on a plate and pour the beans on the toast.

Additions Fred has tried which are not recommended include: (a) chili powder (no amount of chili powder will get you to the goal of chili if where you started was baked beans); (b) curry; (c) chutney. These additions are still less successful when tried all at once.

A good deal of mustard, however, can counteract or somewhat conceal or distract from the above mistakes.

Nicholas Kilmer's mysteries *O Scared Head, Harmony in Flesh and Black,* and *Dirty Linen*, feature Fred Taylor.

Jim Christensen's Macaroni and Guilt
MARTIN J. SMITH

*A*s the lead parent in an unorthodox household, memory expert Jim Christensen, struggles constantly to balance proper nutrition for his two daughters and his lover's young son against the forces of evil against which he occasionally must battle. And as with many overextended parents, Christensen's willingness to compromise increases depending on the severity of the crisis at hand. Typical though his lapses may be, Christensen always feels guilty. And considering the sociopathic menace he sometimes faces, he should easily be forgiven. One final note for those readers who recall the product-tampering scare in *Time Release*: Always check packaging and safety seals before using any off-the-shelf product.

Boil 6 cups of water.

Open familiar blue-orange box of macaroni and cheese.

Stir in the macaroni and boil 7 to 10 minutes, stirring as time permits.

Drain the macaroni—do not rinse—and return to pan.

Add ¼ cup of margarine, ¼ cup of milk, and the powdered cheese-sauce mix; mix well.

Makes about 3 cups.

Note: For nutritional balance, this recipe can be supplemented with carrot sticks (*"Orange food is good for your eyes or something, isn't it?"—Shadow Image*), microwaved hot dogs, or apple slices.

Memory expert Jim Christensen appears in Martin J. Smith's Anthony-nominated *Time Release*, and its sequel, *Shadow Image*.

Koko's Cupcakes

LILIAN JACKSON BRAUN

*L*ilian Jackson Braun graciously provided *A Taste of Murder* with this favorite treat of *The Cat Who...* Then we started thinking, what if....

Koko and Yum Yum had spent most the day doing something highly unusual: sleeping. Qwilleran, stroking his mustache in bewilderment, might wonder, *What is wrong with my usually very feisty feline housemates?* Two cats who barely sat still while savoring one of their many favorite human meals now appeared dead to the world. Perhaps too many crime-free months had caused them to revert back to "normal?"

Not wishing them to lose their nose for crime, Qwilleran might decide to whip up a treat with hopes of bringing them back to reality. As the water boils, Koko might suddenly appear and begin playfully swatting at the round container of rolled oats. Well, it's a start.

> 2 pounds pork livers
> Water
> 2 tablespoons wheat germ
> 2 tablespoons salad oil
> Pinch of dried mint (catnip will do)
> Raw rolled oats

Boil the livers in water to cover until tender. Puree in a blender or whatever. Blend in wheat germ, oil, and mint. Remove to a bowl. Stir in enough rolled oats to make a thick paste. Spoon into muffin cups and freeze.

1 cupcake (thawed to room temperature) serves 2 cats.

Lilian Jackson Braun's hugely successful series of feline mysteries featuring Jim Qwilleran and his two lovable Siamese sidekicks, Koko and Yum Yum, includes *The Cat Who Read Backwards*, *The Cat Who Sang for the Birds*, and *The Cat Who Saw Stars*.

Tivoli Shrimps

DIANA DEVERELL

$\mathcal{B}$orrowing from my own Foreign Service background, my heroine, Casey Collins, works for the U.S. State Department as an analyst on counterterrorism issues. In each book, she's drawn into dangerous field operations by her old friend, Colonel Holger Sorensen, a versatile Scandinavian who works for the Danish Defense Intelligence Service and also serves as pastor of a Lutheran parish north of Copenhagen.

After a successful mission (and when you're a resourceful American woman whose partner is both a military officer and a man of God, odds favor success), Holger and Casey enjoy a festive Danish lunch of smorrebrod, akvavit and ol—open-face sandwiches served with shots of the ice-cold liquor and tall glasses of lager. My fictional characters enjoy marinated herring on rye topped with curry sauce but I find most Americans prefer this recipe:

Lightly butter a thin slice of French bread.

Top with a double layer of small, fresh, cooked shrimp (Pacific shrimp are perfect). Remember to place the shrimps facing the same way, tails outward. Garnish with a lemon wedge and a spear of fresh dill.

After first tasting the sandwich, lift your filled akvavit glass, catch the eye(s) of your dinner partner(s) and say, "Skål." Drain your glass and hold the empty toward your partner in salute to your friendship and drinking stamina. Then soothe your gastrointestinal tract with a long swallow from a great Danish beer.

Diana Deverell has written *12 Drummers Drumming* and *Night on Fire*.

Pemmican

BEVERLY CONNOR

The North American Indians made a dish called pemmican, which they carried with them when traveling because it lasted forever. It was made from dried and pulverized venison or buffalo meat, wild cherries (or other berries), and nuts, mixed with heated animal fat. Below is a modernized version of pemmican more suitable to our culinary sensibilities, which I dug out of my archaeology-class notes from years ago. This is a good food to take hiking and camping.

> 1 cup beef jerky
> 1 cup raisins or dried fruit of choice
> 1 cup crushed pecans, walnuts, or peanuts
> 2 teaspoons honey
> ¼ cup peanut butter

Pound the dried meat to a mealy powder. (You can buy jerky at the grocery store rather than drying the meat yourself.)

Add the dried fruit and nuts.

Heat the honey and peanut butter until softened (don't overcook!).

Mix all the ingredients together thoroughly.

Shape into bars with your hands when cooled.

Place in a plastic bag and store in a cool, dry place (lasts for months).

Beverly Connor writes the Lindsay Chamberlain archaeology mystery series, which includes *A Rumor of Bones*, *Questionable Remains*, and *Dressed to Die*.

PASTA MORTEM

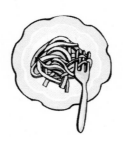

Irene Kelly's Favorite Asparagus Linguine

JAN BURKE

I'm not sure if Irene got this Italian recipe from Lydia or Rachel or Pete, but she loves it. If you are feeding carnivores, start by stir-frying thin strips of chicken or steak (or brown and drain ground beef), then add to the recipe below.

½ pound linguine
1 pound asparagus (thin spears)
1 tablespoon olive oil
1 clove garlic
½ cup green onion
1 14.5-ounce can of diced tomatoes
2 tablespoon Italian herbs (prepackaged, or your own mixture of chopped
    marjoram, thyme, rosemary, oregano, and basil)
Salt
Pepper
½ cup freshly grated Romano or Parmesan cheese (optional)

Cook noodles, rinse, and drain.

Break the woody ends from the asparagus and cut in diagonal slices about 2 inches long, leaving the tips whole. Heat the olive oil in a large skillet over medium heat. Add the asparagus and, stirring constantly, cook until crisp but tender (color should still be bright green). Add the garlic, onions, diced tomatoes, and seasonings. Add the noodles. Toss together just until heated, add cheese if desired.

Makes 4 to 5 servings.

Jan Burke's Irene Kelly mysteries include *Good Night, Irene, Dear Irene,* and *Liar.*

Pasta Crisi

(Crisis Pasta)

CAMILLA CRESPI

*T*his recipe is featured in *The Trouble with Too Much Sun*, in which Simona Griffo finds herself in charge of a publicity shoot on the island of Guadeloupe. I'd been to a few Club Meds and thought the idyllic setting would be a great backdrop for a murder. Plus I needed a vacation badly.

⅓ cup olive oil
2 cloves garlic, minced
¼ teaspoon red pepper flakes
8 sun-dried tomato halves (packed in olive oil), drained and chopped
1 large mozzarella, diced
2 pounds ripe plum tomatoes, thickly sliced lengthwise
Salt and pepper to taste
½ bunch arugula, leaves torn into small pieces (substitute watercress if
  arugula not available)
1 pound imported dried penne or spaghetti

Heat the broiler.

In a large serving bowl, mix the olive oil, garlic, red pepper flakes, sun-dried tomatoes, and mozzarella.

When the broiler is very hot, line the fresh tomato slices on an aluminum-wrapped broiler pan, season with salt and pepper, and broil the tomatoes until their edges turn black—about 10 minutes approximately. (Repeat this process if the pan is not large enough to accommodate all the slices.)

Add the broiled tomato slices to a serving bowl. Add the arugula. This sauce can be prepared a few hours ahead of time. Best served at room temperature.

Cook the pasta in a large pot filled with salted boiling water. When the pasta is al dente, drain and transfer to a serving bowl. Toss all the ingredients together, letting the hot pasta soften the mozzarella.

Eat and forget this crisis!

Serves 4 as a main course.

Camilla Crespi writes the Simona Griffo mysteries, which include *The Trouble with Thin Ice*, *The Trouble with a Bad Fit*, and *The Trouble with a Hot Summer*.

Stanley's Head Pesto

PARNELL HALL

*T*his recipe comes from the Stanley Hastings novel *Scam*, in which, near the end of the book, Stanley's wife Alice makes pesto while they discuss the case. Stanley is somewhat upset because a crooked cop has framed him for three murders. Alice, who is often more insightful than Stanley, is offering an alternate explanation. Stanley asks what it is.

> *I was not to know immediately, for olive oil had joined the cheese, basil, pignoli nuts, and garlic, and the Cuisinart switched on again. When the mixture had been blended to perfection, Alice switched the Cuisinart off and said, "What happens next is, whoever he killed first, now he's gotta kill two more. He does that and hangs onto the gun, which he later plants on you."*
>
> *I blinked. "Wait a minute, wait a minute. That didn't happen. The cop planted the gun on me."*
>
> *"Yeah, but what if he didn't? What if it was actually the bartender that did it?"*
>
> *I grimaced. Sighed. "Alice. I don't want to hear the if-my-theories-were-your-theories bit again, but that particular theory is in contradiction of known facts. This cop Belcher happens to be framing me. I can't get away from that."*
>
> *Alice nodded. "That's your problem. You take something as a given and you can't get away from it. Well, fine. Take that as a fact. Now, set is aside and say, if it wasn't true. Because that's what I'm doing here. I'm playing what-if. Now say, if it wasn't true that the cop was framing me, would it be possible that this bartender planted the gun?"*
>
> *"Are you serious?"*
>
> *Alice looked like the next thing to go in the Cuisinart might be my head.*

Fans of Stanley Hastings will be happy to know he survived both the frame-up and the Cuisinart.

1 cup loosely packed basil	½ cup extra virgin olive oil
½ cup pignoli nuts	Stanley's head (optional)
2 cloves garlic, peeled	1 pound fusilli
¾ cup reggiano cheese	

Chop the basil, pignoli, and garlic in Cuisinart. Add the cheese and blend.

Add the olive oil gradually while blending on low speed.

Add Stanley's head. Switch the Cuisinart to high. (For hearty pesto only. Otherwise, skip this step.)

Cook the fusilli, drain, and serve with pesto.

Makes approximately 4 servings. (Slightly more, with Stanley's head.)

Parnell Hall's suspense novels include *Scam, Trial,* and *Strangler.*

How to Cook Pasta without Getting Whacked

ANTHONY BOURDAIN

*P*asta is serious business. Even the humblest of pasta dishes, Pasta Pommodoro, had better be done right if you're cooking for gangsters.

I've been a professional chef in New York City for twenty years. That means I've worked for, and cooked for, my share of wiseguys and what the FBI calls "organized crime associates." I'm also the author of two crime novels dealing with organized crime—*Bone in the Throat* and *Gone Bamboo*— so I've researched the subject, even gotten to know an ex-gangster in hiding, a very nice man and fellow culinarian.

So let's talk about pasta. Step by step. Read carefully…'cause a mistake could mean you get hog-tied, stuffed into a car trunk, and given an unwanted tour of the Fresh Kills Landfill.

The Pasta

Most wiseguys and serious Italian food buffs and chefs I know prefer the dry stuff. That may surprise you—fresh pasta being all the rage—but, I am told that in Italy, the fresh stuff is a novelty, and it is overrepresented here. A nice box of say, DeCecco penne rigata, cooked al dente, is a good start. Put the amount you want in boiling salted water, cook until almost the doneness you desire, and spread it out on a sheet pan or cookie sheet to cool. Do *not* rinse it! You can rub it with a little olive oil if you must, but don't rinse—that washes off all the starch…and starch is good. In fact, save that pot of cooking water—you'll need it.

The Garlic

Do not ever use a garlic press. Do not chop garlic. Never use that garbage they sell prepeeled and chopped in a jar. Remember what I said about landfills and car rides…Take a few cloves of fresh garlic, peel them, and *slice* them, the long way, thin. You've seen *GoodFellas*, right? If you get nervous around knives, use a razor blade.

The Sauce

American tomatoes usually pale next to their Italian cousins. Good Italian restaurants—even if they're getting in good vine-ripened premium-quality tomatoes—use a mix of canned Italian plum tomatoes and fresh ones. The fresh ones should be peeled, seeded, and hulled. Score them, dip them in boiling water for about 50 seconds, remove, dip in ice water—the skin rolls right off like nobody's business. Squeeze out the seeds, and bada-bing bada-boom, you've got your tomatoes.

Next, in some good quality extra virgin olive oil, sauté your sliced garlic until it melts to a translucent loveliness in the pan. Add some sliced onions and sauté until clear. Do *not* burn your garlic! When the onions and garlic are translucent, add your fresh and your canned tomatoes, a little kosher salt, and some fresh cracked black pepper. Simmer for about 20 minutes to half an hour, and at the every end, add a few leaves of fresh basil, sliced thin. Now it's time to chop it up—this is good practice if you're considering making a career of organized crime. Just use a blending wand, a Cuisinart, or a food mill, and run everything through until it's soft. When the sauce is smooth—various degrees of chunkiness are up to you—you can bring it up to a simmer, mount with a little herb oil or even a little butter. You'd be surprised how much butter good Italian restaurants really use! You've got your sauce.

Finishing it Off

In a pan, with a little olive oil, add a little sliced garlic, according to taste, some crushed red pepper flakes, and a few chunks of additional fresh tomato. Add your sauce and simmer. Here comes the important part— adding the pasta: Dunk your blanched pasta back into the hot cooking water until hot, then drag the basket full of pasta over and drop it into the sauce. A little water comes along for the ride? That's a good thing. The starchy water is considered by most pasta pros to be an essential ingredient. Now, remember this: Your pasta, when served, should not be swimming in sauce. The ratio of sauce to pasta is *very* important! Cook the pasta in the sauce until it sucks it up, absorbs almost all of it. Your penne should be able to be *piled* on the plate, not spread out in a watery mess. A lot of chefs I know emulsify the sauce with a shot of olive oil or butter near the end. A little more fresh basil is a good idea right near the end as well. And of course, check seasoning and add salt and pepper as needed. You got this far—you are well on your way to making your bones and can branch out, add olives, pancetta, anchovies, roasted peppers, etc., in the future. Just don't forget—the pasta should be *tossed* in sauce, not drowned or covered in it. Italians like to actually taste the pasta, not just the sauce.

The Cheese

After all this, if you serve that beauty-ful bowl of pasta pommodoro with some prepared sawdust cheese you get at the supermarket… fuhgettaboutit! You're on your way to gettin' clipped…Buy some nice parmigiana reggiano or a ricotta salata or a pecorino romano. Buy a piece, and shave it or grate it yourself—right at the table! Serve with a nice hunk of cibatta bread and some extra virgin to dip it in, maybe a nice glassa wine (Italian of course), and you'll be gettin' yer button in no time.

Chef Anthony Bourdain's crime novels are *Bone in the Throat* and *Gone Bamboo.*

"Tante Louise is undoubtedly sick—no one could be such a diabolical cook and remain in good health."
—Michael Bond, *Monsieur Pamplemousse and the Secret Mission*

Piano Man Pasta with Shrimp and Asparagus

BILL MOODY

I love angel-hair pasta and asparagus, and so does my character, pianist-sleuth Evan Horne. So I thought, why not combine them? This is an easy, quick meal at home or on the road where, authors and musicians often find themselves. Restaurants and coffee shops get old on road trips, so whenever I can, I like to do some light cooking.

> ½ to ¾ pounds fresh asparagus
> Olive oil
> Angel-hair pasta (I recommend Barilla)
> 1 pound baby shrimp
> Grated Parmesan cheese
> Basil
> Salt and pepper

Preheat the oven to 350 degrees while you cut the asparagus stalks into thirds. Cover a baking tray with aluminum foil and pour a small amount of olive oil on the foil. Roll the asparagus pieces in the oil, lightly coating them, and bake for about 15 minutes. Cook the pasta according to the box directions while sautéing the shrimp in olive oil.

Drain the pasta into a large bowl. Stir in the baked asparagus and shrimp. Sprinkle with Parmesan cheese and basil and salt and pepper to taste. Put the Bill Evans Trio on the stereo and serve with a chilled white wine.

Evan Horne and I prefer Chardonnay.

Bird Lives!, *Sound of the Trumpet*, and *Death of a Tenor Man*, are among Bill Moody's Evan Horne mysteries.

Spaghetti Angelica

AILEEN SCHUMACHER

*L*ong before I began an engineering consulting firm with my husband, Richard Blum, we developed this recipe, which is quick, low-fat, vegetarian, *and* cheap.

> 1 cup cottage cheese
> ½ cup (2 ounces) shredded or grated mozzarella cheese
> 2 tablespoons minced fresh parsley
> Salt and ground pepper to taste
> ¼ teaspoon grated nutmeg
> 6 ounces uncooked spaghetti
> 4-ounce undrained can mushrooms (stems and pieces)

Blend all the ingredients except the spaghetti and mushrooms in blender. Add approximately ½ juice from the canned mushrooms. Discard the remaining juice. Cook the spaghetti in boiling salted water until tender. Drain. Return to the same pot it was cooked in. Stir in the remaining ingredients over very low heat and the spaghetti is uniformly coated and the mixture is warm. Serve immediately.

Serves 4.

Aileen Schumacher is a registered professional engineer. Her mysteries include *Engineered for Murder* and *Framework for Death*.

SOMETHING'S FISHY

May's Famous Tuna Casserole

(More or Less by)

DONALD E. WESTLAKE

I have among my published novels a recidivist character named John Dortmunder, whose joys are few and travails many. Whenever life becomes more than usually difficult for John, his faithful companion, May, lightens his spirits by presenting him with his favorite dinner, May's Famous Tuna Casserole. Over the years, the public demand for the recipe for May's Famous Tuna Casserole has been scant and relenting, and so, some years ago, I felt compelled to offer it to the world at large in *Lit à la Carte*, compiled by Rex Beckham.

Since then, the clamor has continued unheard, which makes me delighted to promulgate the recipe for May's Famous Tuna Casserole (concocted, I must admit, with some exceedingly reluctant help—99 percent—from my wife, the writer and otherwise gourmet, Abby Adams) to an even wider audience.

Just so you know, John's other favorite meal is cornflakes with milk and sugar, in the proportion of 1:1:1.

2 cups milk
3 tablespoons butter
2 tablespoons flour
Salt
Pepper
Nutmeg
Cayenne pepper

12-ounce package of egg noodles
2 10-ounce packages frozen,
    chopped spinach
2 large cans white tuna fish
Grated Parmesan cheese
Bread crumbs

Preheat the oven to 375 degrees.

White sauce: Warm the milk in a small saucepan (do not let boil). In a thick-bottomed saucepan, melt 2 tablespoons of butter and stir in the flour. Cook, whisking continuously, for 4 minutes; add the warm milk gradually and cook while stirring until smooth and thick. Season to taste with salt, pepper, nutmeg, and a pinch of cayenne. Use the other tablespoon of butter to grease a 3-quart casserole.

Meanwhile, cook the noodles until barely done in plenty of boiling water. Drain, and immediately toss in the buttered casserole with 2 tablespoons of the white sauce. Defrost the frozen spinach in boiling water; drain and spread on top of the noodles. Drain the tuna and break up chunks. Spread it on top of the spinach.

Pour the remaining sauce over the top of the casserole. Sprinkle with grated cheese and bread crumbs. Bake for 25 minutes or until bubbling and brown.

Serves 6 for lunch or supper.

Donald E. Westlake, one of today's most prolific writers, is the author of the Dortmunder series which includes *Good Behavior*, *The Hot Rock* and *Nobody's Perfect*, as well as other mysteries including *The Ax*.

Fish Pie

ANNE PERRY

*A*fter Anne Perry generously contributed this recipe, *A Taste of Murder* imagined this scenario:

Shadows from the lighted gas lamps on the street below flickered on Inspector Pitt's windows, as the sound of passing carriages and hansoms filled the air. It had been an uneventful day, so he should be free to go soon. Home to Charlotte and a nice warm supper.

Having been raised in a home filled with servants and cooks hadn't dampened his wife's desire to experience the aromas of a kitchen firsthand. (How fortunate for Thomas, since a policeman could hardly afford servants or cooks.) Inspector Pitt knew chances were high that one of his favorite dishes would be awaiting him tonight. Perhaps the savory fish pie with its wonderful white sauce. Donning his overcoat, Pitt dreamily thought of supper and Charlotte, although not necessarily in that order. His reverie was broken by the door of his office bursting open. "There's been a murder in Bethlehem Road, Sir."

1 pound fish (e.g., cod, sole or hake)	1 cup milk
1 pound potatoes, peeled	Salt and pepper to taste
Butter or margarine	Garlic salt to taste
2 eggs	1 teaspoon tartar sauce
Vegetables, to taste (e.g., leeks, peas)	2 tablespoons chopped parsley
1 ½ to 2 tablespoons flour	Grated cheese to taste

Boil the fish in salted water. Skin, bone, and flake and leave aside.

In a separate pot of salted water, boil the potatoes. Mash and cream with margarine or butter. Leave aside.

Hard-boil the eggs and let cool. Slice and leave aside.

If using leeks or other large vegetables, chop them. Steam-cook all vegetables. Leave to cool.

To make a pouring white sauce: Melt 2 tablespoons of butter over low heat, stir with a wooden spoon. Remove from heat. Stir in the flour evenly to prevent lumping. Add the milk gradually, stirring all the time. Add salt and pepper to taste. Put back on low heat and stir all the time till the sauce thickens. Flavor to taste with garlic salt, tartar sauce, and chopped parsley. Beat till glossy.

Preheat the oven to 375 degrees. In a pie dish (or uncovered casserole), arrange the fish and pour in the sauce. Arrange the sliced eggs on top with the vegetables. Spread the creamed potatoes on top and decorate attractively with a fork. Sprinkle with grated cheese to taste. Bake for approximately 30 minutes, till well-cooked through and golden brown on top. (An attractive finish can be made by arranging diced buttered bread pieces around the edge to make crispy croutons.)

Anne Perry is the author of the William Monk series, including *A Breach of Promise* and *The Silent Cry,* and the series featuring Thomas and Charlotte Pitt, including *Ashworth Hall* and *Bedford Square.*

Mama Catoire's Shrimp Étouffée
TONY FENNELLY

My male protagonists, Matt Sinclair and Julian Fortier, speak French and are fantastic cooks. They acquired these abilities from my husband, Richard Catoire, a Cajun from Evangeline Parish.

Richard says he learned to cook from watching his mama, Elena Fontenot Catoire, in the kitchen of their tenant farmhouse. No cookbooks were available then. (Mama never learned to read.) He shares this favorite recipe.

About 2 tablespoons olive oil (to sauté vegetables)
2 cups chopped onion
1 big head garlic, peeled and minced
2 bell peppers, chopped
2 stalks celery, chopped
3 good bay leaves
½ pound butter or more
5 pounds good, fresh shrimp, peeled (cleaned tails)
1 6-ounce can tomato paste
Salt, red pepper, black pepper, and white pepper to taste
½ bunch parsley, minced
1 bunch green onions, chopped
1 to 2 teaspoons flour for a slurry (a slurry is flour dissolved in
    cold water and added as a thickening agent)
1 teaspoon of gumbo filé
3 cups of rice

Heat the olive oil in a Dutch oven or a thick covered pot. Sauté the onion and garlic until they start to take on a little color. (Keep them moving to make sure not to burn the garlic.) Add the bell pepper and celery and continue to sauté until slightly wilted. Push them to the side, then add bay leaves and 2 sticks of butter in the middle of the pot. Put the peeled shrimp in the middle and stir a little to let them get pink and throw some liquid. Then add a little water, if needed, to make the gravy.

Turn the fire low and simmer slowly. Then season, making sure you don't overseason. Add the tomato paste, and when incorporated, reseason after tasting, with salt, red, black and white peppers. Simmer slowly for about 30 minutes, then add parsley and green onions.

If thickening is necessary, add the slurry to the pot, stir slowly and cook another 5 to 10 minutes and turn it off. Sprinkle about 1 teaspoon of filé on top and stir a little. Serve on top of steamed rice and enjoy.

For perfect fluffy, non-stick rice: Pour long-grain rice in a saucepan. Pour in water, swish it around, then pour it off to rinse the rice. Add fresh water till it's twice as high as the level of the rice; add salt and bring it to a boil. Cover the pot, and cook on a low flame for 15 minutes. Turn off and serve.

Tony Fennelly is the author of *1(900) DEAD*, *The Hippie in the Wall*, and *Murder with a Twist*.

Creole Seafood Gumbo

CAROL O'CONNELL

*I*n keeping with your theme of a crime genre cookbook, I stole this recipe from Brennan's Restaurant on Royal Street in New Orleans.

(Actually, it's a handout sheet from a walking tour. I was investigating local cemeteries as research for *Stone Angel*. The recipe led me to Brennan's and the best meal of my life.)

But let's say I stole it. Because I'm a rank amateur at stealing things, I got permission from the Brennan family so that I might contribute my favorite recipe with a clear conscience.

¼ cup vegetable oil
1 ⅓ cups all-purpose flour
1 large onion, finely chopped
2 celery ribs, finely chopped
6 garlic cloves, finely chopped
½ green bell pepper, finely chopped
16 ounces (2 cups) tomato sauce
16 ounces (2 cups) canned or very ripe fresh peeled tomatoes
1 pound okra, stemmed and sliced into rings
2 bay leaves
⅓ cup Worcestershire sauce
1 ½ teaspoons salt
1 teaspoon black pepper
1 ½ quarts cold water
2 cups (about 48) shucked oysters
4 pounds medium shrimp, peeled and deveined
4 boiled hard-shell crabs, broken in half and gills removed
8 ounces lump crabmeat, picked over to remove any shell and cartilage
1 tablespoon filé powder
5 cups cooked white rice

First make a roux by heating the oil in a heavy skillet, then blending in the flour. Cook over a low to medium heat until brown, about 10 to 12 minutes. Add the onion, celery, garlic, and bell pepper and sauté until tender, about 5 minutes. Add the tomato sauce and tomatoes and cook 20 minutes longer. Add the okra, bay leaves, Worcestershire, salt, and pepper, along with 1 ½ quarts cold water. Cover the pot and cook over medium heat until the okra is tender, about 20 to 30 minutes. Stir in the oysters, shrimp, and crabs, reduce the heat and simmer several minutes, until the shrimp are cooked through.

Just before serving, remove the bay leaves and add the lump crabmeat and filé powder. Heat the gumbo briefly, until the crabmeat is warm, then spoon into bowls over hot cooked white rice.

Serves 10 to 12.

Carol O'Connell is the author of *Judas Child* and the Kathleen Mallory series, including *The Man Who Cast Two Shadows* and *Mallory's Oracle*.

Sole Hitchcock

(A Mystery Lover's Classic)

*T*his "off-the-menu" item from the legendary Chasen's in Los Angeles, where Alfred Hitchcock dined every Thursday night for forty years (and where he outlined the plot for *Notorious* during one such dinner), was the master of suspense's favorite. As they say, it's all in the sauce.

    4 8-ounce fillets, sole (preferably Dover) or flounder
    Salt and pepper to taste
    All-purpose flour, as needed
    2 whole eggs
    Cracker crumbs, as needed (preferably Ritz brand or saltines)
    4 tablespoons butter
    Duglere sauce (recipe follows)

Preheat the oven to 450 degrees. Clean, bone, and trim the fish. Season with salt and pepper. Coat the fish with flour, dip in beaten eggs and coat with cracker crumbs. Shake off excess. In a skillet over medium heat, sauté fish in butter until golden brown on both sides. Place in a preheated oven for 10 minutes to finish cooking.

Remove from pan and transfer to a warm plate. Serve with Duglere Sauce.

Serves: 4

Duglere Triple Sauce

Chicken Cream Sauce

    3 tablespoons butter
    3 tablespoons all-purpose flour
    $\frac{1}{4}$ cup chicken broth
    $\frac{1}{2}$ cup heavy whipping cream
    $\frac{1}{2}$ teaspoon lemon juice
    $\frac{1}{2}$ teaspoon Worcestershire sauce
    Salt and pepper to taste

Melt the butter in a medium saucepan and stir in the flour. Stir in the broth and cream all at once. Cook and stir until the mixture comes to a boil. Reduce heat, simmer 2 minutes more. Mix in lemon juice, Worcestershire sauce, and salt and pepper to taste. Remove from heat.

Tomato Sauce

2 tablespoons butter
¼ cup onion, chopped
1 ½ cups tomato puree
1 ½ cups tomatoes, chopped
1 tablespoon fresh basil, minced
1 tablespoon fresh oregano, minced
½ teaspoon salt
¼ teaspoon pepper

Melt the butter in a large skillet. Sauté the onion in butter until tender. Stir in the tomato puree, chopped tomatoes, basil, oregano, salt and pepper. Simmer uncovered over low heat for 15 minutes or until reduced to desired consistency. Puree if desired.

Makes about 3 cups.

Duglere Sauce

4 teaspoons butter
4 teaspoons shallots, minced
1 cup fresh tomatoes, chopped
Salt and pepper to taste
1 tablespoon chives, minced.

Heat the butter in a heavy saucepan over medium heat. Add the shallots and tomatoes and sauté until they are slightly softened. Season with salt and pepper. Add 1 cup of the chicken cream sauce and 2 tablespoons of the tomato sauce. Simmer. Sprinkle with chives and serve the sauce at room temperature.

Sea Bass In Orange Sauce

(As Prepared for Him by His Personal Chef, Holly Erickson)
RICHARD NORTH PATTERSON

$\mathcal{M}$r. Patterson has asked his personal chef, Holly Erickson, to provide us with a recipe for one of his favorite dishes. According to Ms. Erickson, the Patterson family loves fish and savors seafood whether in San Francisco or Martha's Vineyard. This summery dish with its light flavors is actually easy to prepare year-round because the ingredients are available every season.

Zest of 1 orange
6 or so tablespoons butter (or if you prefer, mild olive oil)
1 brown onion, chopped
1 cup good white Italian wine
    (use the wine you'd like to drink with the meal)
Juice of 4 oranges
Italian parsley, chopped (save some for garnish)
6 fillets sea bass (or trout or snapper)
Flour for dredging
Salt and pepper to taste

Boil the zest of the orange for about 5 minutes. Remove and drain. Melt half the butter, and sweat the onion until it is soft, fragrant and translucent. Add the wine, orange juice, orange zest, and some chopped parsley, and heat until somewhat reduced. Meanwhile, dredge the fish in flour and salt and pepper. Sauté the fish in the remaining butter (or oil). Three minutes per side is the rule, but break it if you like your fish well-cooked.

Place the cooked fish on plates and pour the orange sauce over it. Garnish with parsley and orange slices.

Richard North Patterson's mystery novels include *Silent Witness*, *The Lasko Tangent* and *No Safe Place*.

Justin's Tuna Steaks

LINDA FAIRSTEIN

Like her creator, Alexandra Cooper is a prosecutor in the New York County District Attorney's Office. But since the books are fiction, I took the liberty of making Alex younger, thinner, and blonder than I am. I also endowed her with a trust fund, so that she was able to buy a wonderful old farmhouse on Martha's Vineyard, which is the setting for *Final Jeopardy*, and to which Alex returns throughout the series.

One other trait which Alex and I share is our dislike of cooking. We both love great food, but our busy and unpredictable work schedules make it awfully difficult to get home at a reasonable hour to prepare and cook a decent meal. So like me, Alex spends a lot of time in restaurants or relying on a microwaved Lean Cuisine dinner alone.

When Alex finally settles down in a significant relationship, I have my fingers crossed that the guy she winds up with enjoys creating culinary masterpieces as much as the man I married does. It allows me to continue doing the two things I like best professionally, writing and prosecuting, yet still sit down to a delicious feast at the end of the day.

I do most of my writing at our home on Martha's Vineyard, so I have chosen a recipe of my husband's that has sustained me after many long hours of writing on an August day and that will appear in a forthcoming Alexandra Cooper novel.

It's the main course in what I would consider a traditional Vineyard summer meal. We'd begin by serving clam chowder, and then, along with native island corn and a superb local tomato and red onion salad, the special dish would be Justin's tuna steaks.

3 pounds fresh tuna, cut into ¾-inch steaks (This works with any firm-fleshed fish.)

Marinade:

⅓ cup Dijon mustard	2 teaspoons salt
⅓ cup lemon juice	1 teaspoon ground black pepper
3 tablespoons fresh rosemary	Melted butter to taste
1 ⅓ cups virgin olive oil	Rosemary sprigs for garnish
2 cloves garlic, minced	Lemon wedges for garnish

Mix all the marinade ingredients in a bowl and, using a food processor, puree for 30 seconds until creamy and smooth. Pour the marinade in a glass or stainless-steel casserole. Place the tuna steaks in the marinade, making sure they are completely covered with the sauce. Marinade at room temperature for 1 hour.

Cooking time on grill or broiler is about 4 minutes per side.

Reserve the marinade. After cooking, keep the fish warm, and mix the sauce with melted butter to taste. Then, cover the fish again with this marinade, serving the rest on the side. Garnish with rosemary sprigs and lemon wedges.

In addition to *Final Jeopardy*, Alexandra Cooper also appears in *Likely to Die* and *Cold Hit*.

Almost Patented Teriyaki Salmon

JOHN T. LESCROART

$\mathcal{I}$n my novel *The 13th Juror* is the following passage:

> The previous Monday (Dismas) Hardy and his brother-in-law Moses (McGuire) had gone salmon fishing off the Marin Coast. They'd caught two each. That night, at Moses' apartment, they'd roasted one for dinner. A second—the sixteen-pounder they were going to have that night—they'd put in some of Moses' nearly patented home-made teriyaki sauce to marinate. The other two they filleted, rubbed with rock salt, sugar, and cognac, packed with some peppercorns and brown sugar, wrapped in foil and weighted down with bricks in Hardy's refrigerator. They intended to eat gravlax until they didn't want to anymore or died, whichever came first.

So herewith, Moses McGuire's Almost Patented Teriyaki Salmon. It is really outstanding.

> 2 pound salmon fillets (not steaks), skin on
> Juice of 1 lemon
> ½ cup soy sauce
> 1 teaspoon dried thyme
> 2 tablespoons extra virgin olive oil
> Fresh tarragon and thyme, chopped
> Butter

Mix the lemon juice, soy sauce, dried thyme, and olive oil in a wide, shallow container, and place the fillets skin side up into the marinade. Let stand at least an hour, but refrigerated overnight is better. Prepare the barbecue (Weber kettle barbecue is great.) When the coals are ready and very hot, oil the grill lightly, then place the fillets skin side *down* directly on the grill. If using a kettle grill, cover. If not, cover with aluminum-foil tent and watch for flames. *Do not turn the fish over.* Cook at least 6 minutes but no more than 10. The salmon should be orange/pink at the surface, with the skin quite burned. Dot with softened butter into which you've beaten fresh chopped tarragon and thyme. If desired, heat the marinade to boiling, and serve as additional sauce for dipping or for rice, etc.

Serves 4.

John Lescroart is the author of *The 13th Juror*, *The Vig*, and *Dead Irish*.

Yellowtail à la Deal

LES STANDIFORD

*H*ere's a typical John Deal meal, as inspired by those comments in *Presidential Deal* where our guy laments that he'd far rather be at his favorite bayside restaurant, The Red Fish Grill in Miami, eating yellowtail and drinking Jamaican Red Stripe beer than finding himself drawn into the line of big trouble once again.

Yellowtail à la Deal works best with the fillet of that most delicate of all the snapper types, but red snapper will do, and, in a pinch, so will any thin-filleted and flaky white fish, even. Coat a medium-size fry pan with peanut oil, and heat until it sizzles when you drop a bead of water in it. Shred a couple tablespoons' worth of fresh coconut into the oil, stir for a moment, then add the fish. Squeeze a lime or a lemon half over the fish, and sprinkle on some spice that will get their attention. Deal and I use K-Paul's Cajun and a little green Tabasco. Turn the fish over (this won't take long if the fish is thin and you heated the pan the way you were supposed to), and repeat the lime/lemon/spice process.

Deal and I like to remove the fish, which will be slightly seared if things are working out right, directly out of the pan onto a bed of wild rice, with a side of yellow/red/green peppers and red onion chunks that have been lightly sautéed in olive oil with a couple tablespoons of crushed garlic (or, better yet, marinate these vegetables briefly in oil and crushed garlic, then toss them on the grill until they're cooked to your taste, which shouldn't be too long). Shred a little more fresh coconut on things and give everyone their own chunk of lemon or lime to use for seasoning.

Some salad is always good, too. Deal likes to whip up a simple vinaigrette, 3:1 cold-pressed olive oil to red vinegar, with a little lemon pepper and a teaspoon of sugar. Use a mechanical beater or, if you're more coordinated than Vernon Driscoll, a whisk, so that you feel more like a pro. Tear up some red or Bibb lettuce, wash it well, and chill it, then toss with the dressing.

Driscoll would always wash this down with the aforementioned Red Stripe, and Deal often would too, but if Janice had agreed to come for dinner, he might spring for a decent Chardonnay, one with a little bite, like J. Lohr Estate or Estancia.

I'd recommend Key lime pie for dessert, but if you think I can pry that recipe loose from Deal, you're an optimistic sort. You want good Key lime pie, you're going to have to come to the Keys.

Les Standiford's John Deal mysteries include *Raw Deal, Done Deal,* and *Deal on Ice.*

Heavenly Halibut

SISTER CAROL ANNE O'MARIE

Sister Mary Helen, seventies-plus retired nun teaching at San Francisco's Mount St. Francis College, makes a habit of solving murders. One of her favorite dishes on meatless Fridays (especially during Lent) is this Heavenly Halibut.

> 16 ounces halibut steaks
> Salt and pepper
> ⅓ cup dry white wine
> ½ onion, sliced
> ½ cup sliced celery
> 4 tablespoons butter (can substitute olive oil)
> 1 tablespoon parsley
> 1 teaspoon Worcestershire sauce
> ⅓ teaspoon dried basil, crushed
> 1 cup halved cherry tomatoes

Sprinkle the fish with salt and pepper. Place in a shallow dish. Add the wine. Let it stand 30 minutes, turning once.

In a medium skillet, cook the onions and celery in butter (or olive oil) until tender, not brown. Stir in parsley, Worcestershire sauce, and basil. Add the fish and wine.

Cover and cook over low heat until the fish is almost done, about 10 minutes. Add the cherry tomatoes. Cover and cook 3 to 4 minutes, until the fish flakes.

Serves 2 to 4.

Sister Carol Anne O'Marie's books include *A Novena for Murder*, *Murder Makes a Pilgrimage*, and *The Missing Madonna*.

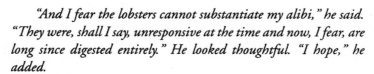

"And I fear the lobsters cannot substantiate my alibi," he said. "They were, shall I say, unresponsive at the time and now, I fear, are long since digested entirely." He looked thoughtful. "I hope," he added.
—Frances and Richard Lockridge, *The Norths Meet Murder*

Fish Fillets With Crabmeat Stuffing

LINDA FRENCH

In Talking Rain, *the doltish wrestler Steamboat gradually reveals himself to be a very urbane and accomplished fellow. One of his talents is gourmet cooking, and this is the way he uses two wonderful ingredients available right outside the door at March Hunt's floating cabin on the remote west coast of Vancouver Island:*

> *They all worked busily for twenty minutes, gradually finding themselves lured inside by the transcendent smells from the kitchen. Standing in front of the great Monarch stove with a blue-checked dish towel across his chest, Steamboat deftly mixed sautéed onions*, crabmeat, and bread crumbs for stuffing. Packing the mixture into rockfish fillets, he cinched them with marjoram twigs plucked from March's rafters.*

*Steamboat used sautéed onions because he didn't have baby green ones.

> 4 medium-size fillets of any good white fish, red snapper (rockfish) preferred
> Salt and pepper to taste
> 1 3-ounce can of crabmeat or shrimp. (Of course, fresh is even better)
> ¾ cup bread crumbs
> ½ cup chopped green onions
> 3 tablespoons light olive oil (or butter, melted, if your heart can afford it)
> Paprika (optional)
> Water, if necessary

Season the fillet with salt and pepper. Preheat the oven to 350 degrees.

Mix the crabmeat, bread crumbs, and green onions together, adding enough oil (or melted butter) to help hold it together and a little water, if necessary. Pat the crabmeat stuffing on 2 fillets, then lay the other 2 fillets on top, making crabmeat "sandwiches." Pin together with toothpicks or festive skewers; drizzle with a little oil or butter. Sprinkle on a bit more salt and pepper (and paprika, if you like). Place in an ovenproof baking dish. Bake for about 15 minutes. Do not overcook the fillets, and if fillets are of uniform thickness to begin with, you'll have less trouble getting everything done at the same time.

Cut the fillets in half at the table.

Serves 4.

Linda French is the author of mysteries centered in the Pacific Northwest including *Talking Rain* and *Coffee to Die For.*

Beer-Battered Walleye
KATHLEEN TAYLOR

A longtime resident of South Dakota, my amateur sleuth, the overweight, over-forty, widowed waitress Tory Bauer, lives in the tiny rural fictional town of Delphi. The nearby Missouri River is chock-full of walleye which is a mean-tempered fish with lots of sharp teeth. However the wily walleye cooks up marvelously.

Several walleye fillets, cleaned, boned, washed, and patted dry,
 and cut into approximately 1 ½-by-1-inch pieces
Oil
1 egg
¼ cup evaporated milk
½ cup warm flat beer (any brand)
2 cups fine cracker crumbs
1 teaspoon onion salt
1 teaspoon garlic salt
1 teaspoon celery salt
1 teaspoon pepper

Preheat the oil to 375 degrees in a deep-fat fryer.

In a bowl, whisk the egg, milk, and beer together. In a separate bowl, combine the dry ingredient. Note: Spices can be added or subtracted to taste. Dip dry the walleye chunks in egg-milk mixture. Roll the dipped walleye chunks in the crumb mixture. Deep-fat fry in preheated oil for 3-5 minutes, or until golden brown. Drain on paper towels. Serve with lemon wedges, tartar or cocktail sauce. (Occasionally, skim the crumbs from the oil, and make sure that the oil temperature returns to 375 degrees between batches.)

Kathleen Taylor's sleuth, Tory Bauer, has made an appearance in *Sex and Salmonella*, *The Hotel South Dakota* and *Funeral Food*, to name a few.

How to Eat a Maryland Blue Crab

BARBARA LEE

*I*f you are from Maryland, you will know that dead man's fingers are the gills of Maryland's famous blue crabs. Parents tell their kids not to eat the dead man. *Dead Man's Fingers* offers a lesson in how to eat a crab. I wrote it to amuse myself and to amuse my editor, Ruth Cavin, who loves blue crabs and doesn't need any lessons in how to eat them.

Alas, both my sleuth, Eve Elliott, and I are New Yorkers, and both of us had to learn to eat crabs. Actually, Eve has never cooked a meal in her life, and if you requested a recipe, she'd tell you how to make toast. Fortunately, handsome men are forever offering to buy her dinner or cooking for her. One teaches her to eat crabs.

Order a dozen Jumbos or #1 Jimmys (males). They usually come covered with Old Bay seasoning. You eat them sitting at long tables covered with brown paper, preferably on a deck overlooking the water. You need a thick mallet and knife. Napkins. Beer. A couple of hours, since crab eating can't be hurried. Here's how it's done:

a) Snap off the legs and put the corpse aside. Snap the legs in half at jointed cartilage.

b) Pound the legs gently with mallet, then tease out the meat.

c) Turn the big flat corpse over. Put your thumb or a knife under the apron (looks like a pop-top) and pry off. Pull the crab apart and discard the pop-top side.

d) Yikes: The dead man's fingers. Get rid of them quick.

e) Yellowish-green gunk is caviar and can be eaten on crackers. Or not.

f) Snap the crab in half and then in quarters. Root around for the meat with your fingers.

If you want to steam crabs at home, here is what I've seen friends do:

In large pot, with a rack and tight lid, layer a dozen large crabs with a commercial seasoning such as Old Bay. (Crabs, seasoning, more crabs.) Cover with a mixture of vinegar, beer, and water to taste. Steam for 20 or 30 minutes until crabs turn bright red.

I've never done this. (Remember *Annie Hall?*)

In addition to *Dead Man's Fingers*, Barbara Lee has also written *Death in Still Waters*.

Seafood Bledsonia

JERRY BLEDSOE

I had intended offering here my famous recipe for Left-handed Whelk Chowder, which I used to cook every year at the Strange Seafood Festival at the Hampton Mariners Museum in Beaufort, North Carolina. This dish was rightly famous and proclaimed by far the best at the festival by all who tasted it, which may not be a great compliment considering that the other choices ranged from mole-crab soup and eel-on-a-spit to steamed marsh snails and sea-kale salad. Alas, though, whelks of all persuasions are verging on becoming endangered, and the already rare left-handed whelk is now almost impossible to find. Therefore, I offer another seafood dish, this one famous only among my friends. One taste and you will sing my praises forever. I call it Seafood Bledsonia because I once had a dish at an Italian restaurant that the owner had named after himself. His name was Anthony, and he called his dish Seafood Antonia. My dish and his aren't much alike (mine is decidedly superior), but I named mine after his because I just liked the way that *nia* sounded at the end of Bledsoe.

I should warn you that this definitely is a "rich" dish, costly to prepare, and definitely not for the calorie-conscious or cholesterol-wary. Please note, too, that I never use measurement when cooking, so those offered are only approximations and you are free to tinker with them to suit your own tastes.

2 cups rice
1 large sweet red pepper
½ pound firm white fish (grouper or red snapper)
2 lobster tails (preferably Maine lobster, but the so-called tropical lobster,
    which is really a big crayfish, will do)
1 pound crabmeat (any will do, but lump blue crab is best)
½ pound shrimp
½ pound scallops (preferably bay scallops)
½ pound butter
1 tablespoon flour
16 ounces clam juice
1 pint cream
¼ cup sherry
½ pound Swiss cheese, shredded
½ pound mozzarella cheese, shredded
½ pound freshly grated Parmesan cheese

Steam the rice. Roast the pepper in the oven; remove the skin and dice. Remove the skin from the fish and cut into chunks. Cut the lobster tails into chunks. Pick the crabmeat to remove all the shell and cartilage. Melt 1 stick of butter in a large saucepan over low heat so that it doesn't brown. Sauté the fish, lobster, shrimp, and scallops until translucence is gone. Do not overcook. Remove to a side dish, leaving the butter in the pan. Add the crabmeat to the butter and warm. In another saucepan, make a roux of flour and the other stick of butter, being careful not to brown it. Slowly add the clam juice and cream until the sauce has reached a medium-to-heavy thickness. Add the sherry. Spread the rice to a depth of about ¾ inch in a large baking dish. Cover with the seafood, making a good mix. Dot with diced pepper. Pour the sauce over this and top with cheeses. Place in 350-degree oven until the cheeses begin to brown.

The author of 15 books, Jerry Bledsoe is best known for his best-selling true-crime chronicles, including *Bitter Blood, Death Sentence* and *Before He Wakes.*

Coquilles St. Jacques

BONNIE MACDOUGAL

*T*his recipe plays a key element in the plot of *Breach of Trust*, in that it helps bolster Scott Sterling's alibi for the murder of Curtis Mason. In essence, the heroine, Jennifer Lodge, believes he must be innocent because he cooked and served Coquilles St. Jacques the night of the murder, and she knows he must have spent an hour or two in the kitchen. (Later she learns that he actually got it at a take-out French restaurant).

Here it is.

Bring ¾ cup of dry white wine to a boil in a wide skillet. Add 1 ½ pounds of scallops, rinsed, drained, and cut into ¾-inch chunks. Cover and cook on medium-low heat 3 or 4 minutes, until the scallops are opaque. Lift the scallops from the pan with a slotted spoon and set aside. Measure the remaining liquid, and either reduce to 1 cup or add water to reach 1 cup.

In the same pan, melt 3 tablespoons of butter and cook ¾ pound of sliced mushrooms on high heat, until all the liquid is absorbed. Stir in 2 tablespoons of flour and remove the pan from the heat. Slowly add the reserved liquid and bring to a boil, stirring until thickened. Reduce heat to medium and stir in 1 cup of shredded Gruyere cheese. Return the scallops to the sauce; add salt to taste.

Spoon the mixture into 4 scallop shells or 1-cup casseroles. Sprinkle ¼ cup of shredded Gruyere over the top. Bake uncovered in a 400-degree oven for 15 to 20 minutes or until the sauce bubbles.

Makes 4 servings.

Bonnie MacDougal is the author of *Breach of Trust* and *Angle of Impact*.

Owl play

Sarah's Easy Mexican Casserole

CAROLYN G. HART

*T*his recipe is my favorite meal that my daughter, Sarah Winchester, always fixes for me when I visit her, and she's given it to me for this collection. Annie Lawrence Darling's dizzy mother-in-law, Laurel, might not be as easily satisfied.

    3 cups grated Monterey Jack cheese
    1 cup grated cheddar cheese
    1 bunch scallions, chopped
    1 tablespoon vegetable oil
    3 10-ounce cans cooked chicken, shredded
    1 8-ounce can tomato juice
    1 15-ounce can tomato sauce
    1 14.5-ounce can whole peeled tomatoes, diced, undrained
    8-ounce can corn
    1 1.25-ounce package taco seasoning
    ½ teaspoon oregano
    ½ teaspoon cumin
    18 medium corn tortillas
    1 4-ounce can pitted black olives, drained and sliced

Helpful hint: Approximately ¾ pound of Monterey Jack equals 3 cups, grated, and approximately ⅓ pound of cheddar equals 1 cup, grated.

Preheat the oven to 350 degrees. In a bowl, gently stir the 2 cheeses together; set aside. In a large skillet, sauté the scallions in oil. Add the chicken, tomato juice, tomato sauce, tomatoes, corn, taco seasoning, and spices. Blend well. Bring to a boil, reduce heat, simmer uncovered for 15 minutes. Place in 13-by-2-by-9-inch glass baking dish *or* 4 disposable foil loaf pans (see note, below). Layer beginning with 4 tortillas, ⅓ of the chicken spread over the tortillas, ⅓ of the olives sprinkled about, and ⅓ of the cheese mixture. Repeat the layers twice. Bake at 350 degrees for 20 minutes or until warm and bubbly.

Serves 10 to 12.

Note: This is a great make-ahead-and-freeze dish. Sarah uses loaf pans to freeze in smaller quantities.

Carolyn G. Hart is the author of two different mystery series: Annie Lawrence Darling appears in *Death on Demand, Honeymoon with Murder* and *Mint Julep Murder*; and the Henrie O series includes *Death on the River Walk, Death in Paradise* and *Death in Lovers' Lane.*

Freni Hostetler's Chicken and Dumplings

TAMAR MYERS

$\mathcal{M}$y mother's family has been Amish for at least three hundred years. All her forebears immigrated to the United States from Switzerland in the early 1700s, and all were Amish. I like to believe that my recipe came with my six-times great-grandfather, Jacob Hochstetler (his wife's name is unrecorded) on the *Charming Nancy* in 1738. Likewise, I wish to believe that the recipe survived the Northkill Amish settlement massacre by the Delaware in 1757. Alas, poor Jacob's wife was stabbed in the back and scalped during that attack, but he and several children survived. Jacob and two of his sons, including my five-times great-grandfather, were captured by the Indians and officially adopted into the tribe. They were later released at the close of the French and Indian War.

I know for a fact that my mother, who became a Mennonite as a young girl, took the recipe with her to Africa in 1932. She and my father were missionaries in a remote area of the Belgian Congo, and that's where I was born and raised. Elephant, hippo, Cape buffalo, and even monkey were part of our diet, but on rare occasions Mama would get her hands on a scrawny little chicken and made the dumpling recipe.

The recipe was included in my first mystery, *Too Many Crooks Spoil the Broth*.

2 chickens (year-old hens preferred)	3 large carrots, sliced
1 ½ teaspoons salt	1 large onion, chopped
Dash black pepper	4 tablespoons chopped parsley
6 medium-size potatoes, quartered	

Clean and pluck the hens. Give the head, entrails, and feet to barn cats. Do what you want with the liver, stomach, and gizzard. Cut the hens into serving pieces and put them into a large, cast-iron pot. Sprinkle with salt and pepper and cover with water. Cook slowly until almost tender. Then skim off the excess fat and foam that has formed on top. Add the vegetables and cook 20 minutes more. Then spoon the dumpling batter (see below) on top of the boiling broth and meat. Cover the kettle tightly and cook 10 more minutes. Do not open the kettle until ready to serve.

3 cups flour	Dash ground nutmeg
1 teaspoon salt	3 eggs, beaten
3 teaspoons baking powder	½ cup cream

To make dumplings, sift the dry ingredients together. Then add the beaten eggs and enough cream to make a batter stiff enough to drop from a spoon.

Tamar Myers writes two mystery series. Her Pennsylvania Dutch mysteries, featuring inn owner Magdalena Yoder, include *Eat, Drink and Be Wary* and *Just Plain Pickled to Death*. *So Faux, So Good* and *Baroque and Desperate* are two of her Den of Antiquity series with crime-solving antiques dealer Abigail Timberlake.

Scaloppini Mysteriosa à la Elizabeth Daniels Squire

ELIZABETH DANIELS SQUIRE

*I*f you wish either to accuse someone of fraud or to improve their memory, invite them to an elegant dinner with Scaloppini Mysteriosa. They will assume they are eating veal scaloppini, especially if they happen to be from a Mafia family who knows good food. After they rave about the veal, explain that this recipe is as clever as they are. It's a fraud, with no veal in it. Now that they know you're onto them, perhaps they'll come clean. On the other hand, their line of defense may be that they can't remember. Explain that this recipe has an ingredient that boosts memory: rosemary. Shakespeare said it: *Rosemary, that's for remembrance.*

Peaches Dann, my absentminded sleuth, who uses every memory device there is to help solve murders, might have this scaloppini for forgetful friends. For dessert she'd have fresh fruit—cherries, first choice—and gingko tea. Gingko tea increases the circulation in your brain—and that boosts memory even more than rosemary.

> 3 pounds boned, skinned chicken thighs, divided into 2 or 4 pieces each,
>   depending on size
> ¾ cup flour
> 1 tablespoon thyme
> 1 tablespoon rosemary
> 2 tablespoons paprika
> 2 tablespoons olive oil
> 1 large pat of butter
> 2 to 3 shallots, chopped
> 2 ½ cups chicken stock
> 1 ½ cups Italian (sweet) vermouth
> Cornstarch or arrowroot
> 2 cups half-and-half or evaporated milk
> 1 pound large mushrooms, thinly sliced, including stems
> 2 or 3 roasted red sweet peppers (out of a jar), cut in strips

Pound the pieces of boned chicken thighs gently until they are quite thin. Combine the flour, thyme, rosemary, and paprika; dredge each piece of pounded chicken in the flour mixture and shake off excess. Combine the oil and butter in a large stickproof skillet, brown the chicken lightly over a hot flame, remove from pan, and set aside.

Add the chopped shallots to the pan, adding a little more oil if needed, and sauté until translucent. Do not brown the shallots.

In a separate saucepan, combine the chicken stock and the vermouth; add the shallots. Thicken with arrowroot or cornstarch. Add the half-and-half or evaporated milk.

Meanwhile, in the skillet, sauté the mushrooms lightly in a little more olive oil.

In a lasagna pan or other ovenproof dish, assemble the chicken, the mushrooms, and the sauce. Add the roasted red peppers evenly. At this point, the entire dish may be refrigerated up to 24 hours.

Remove the dish from the refrigerator an hour ahead of time and, when approaching room temperature, put in a hot (400-degree) oven until thoroughly heated and bubbly, but not long enough to curdle the sauce. Total heating time should be 20 to 30 minutes.

Serve with polenta, pasta, or rice, garnished with chopped fresh parsley or cilantro. Add a green salad.

Serves 8. May be expanded or contracted proportionally.

Elizabeth Daniels Squire is the author of *Is There a Dead Man in the House?* and *Whose Death Is It Anyway?*.

Hanna's Baked Chicken Breast Parmesan For Ten

JUDITH VIORST

"I am not the murdering kind, but I am planning to kill Mr. Monti because he is doing harm to my family," confesses Brenda Kovner in *Murdering Mr. Monti*. It seems that Joseph Monti, the menacing father of her son's fiancée, will deploy all-out vendetta tactics to terminate his daughter's engagement. So, even while doling out household hints and planning a Thanksgiving feast for fifteen, Brenda counterattacks Mr. Monti's vicious assaults with her own meddlesome schemes. But, even when planning a murder, consummate mom Brenda always has dinner on the table. This recipe is one of her standbys, just perfect for those times when the kids are in town and no two people can agree on what they should have for dinner. Everyone likes this, especially if they don't know how much butter is in it.

> 4 cups bread crumbs
> 1 ¼ cups grated Parmesan
> Salt and pepper
> 1 ½ cups butter
> Garlic
> 2 ½ tablespoons Dijon mustard
> 1 ½ teaspoons Worcestershire sauce
> 10 boneless, skinless chicken breasts

Combine the bread crumbs, cheese, salt, and pepper. Melt the butter separately; add garlic, mustard, and Worcestershire. Dip the breasts in the butter mixture and then the crumb mix. Pour the remaining butter into a shallow baking dish, place the breasts in the dish. Bake in a 350-degree oven 30 to 45 minutes, turning once.

Serve with crème fraîche sauce (a mixture of sour cream, crème fraîche, mayonnaise, and spices). Or make more butter-mustard sauce.

Serves 10.

After many years writing hugely successful nonfiction books and humorous verse, Judith Viorst wrote her first novel, *Murdering Mr. Monti*.

Port Royal Chicken

LINDA GRANT

*C*atherine Sayler, my private eye, is not a much better cook than I am. She tends to arrive in the kitchen, as I do, late and with no plan of action. The result is often a desperate search of fridge and larder for a reasonable set of ingredients that will spare the cook a trip to the store. This can result in some bizarre combinations, but on occasion, you stumble on a winner.

I took that attitude to Paris with me one September when my husband and I rented a small apartment in the Latin Quarter. The kitchen was tiny, but the offerings of the street market just up the block were too tempting to pass up. Most days, the sidewalk of the Boulevard Port Royal was nothing more than a wide pedestrian walkway, but early Tuesday and Saturday mornings, a fleet of small trucks pulled up to the curb and in less than half an hour transformed the sidewalk into a feast for the senses.

Stalls lined the sidewalk, displaying fruits and vegetables so fresh they might have been picked that morning: white and yellow cheeses labeled with their origins and fat contents; nuts, olives, and dried fruits; freshly baked breads; and fish and other fruits of the sea laid out on beds of ice. One vendor called out to passersby to taste his ripe red strawberries, smaller than their U.S. cousins but richly sweet. Another extolled the virtues of his melons. Handwritten signs identified not only the type of produce but often the province or country of origin.

The first morning I encountered the market, I was so enchanted that I shopped purely on whim. One table displayed about twenty kinds of olives—greens and blacks, tiny ones no larger than kidney beans, fat ones, shriveled ones. Olives flavored with garlic, herbs, cinnamon, citrus, and bits of other fruits and spices I couldn't identify. I chose some large green ones flavored with lemon and orange, and the merchant dumped a generous spoonful into a plastic bag. At the next stall, I picked up a stem of tomatoes—so red and perfect they looked ready for a photo shoot—several handfuls of thin, deep green French beans, a melon round as a ball, and a head of dark green lettuce. From the butcher I bought chicken breasts, and from the cheese stand, slices of several cheeses.

When dinnertime arrived, I surveyed my treasures and decided to see what I could make of them. The olives had a citrus flavor that was at once rich and sharp, strong enough to spice the chicken, so I used them as seasoning; in they went with the tomatoes and some garlic and shallots. The results were a simple but tasty dish that takes less than a half hour to prepare. But be warned: This dish depends entirely on the olives and tomatoes for flavor. Be sure to use imported olives and fresh, ripe tomatoes. The flavor will vary depending on what kind of olives you choose, and if you can't get ones that will impart a strong flavor, you might want to add some fresh tarragon or rosemary.

> 2 to 4 boneless chicken breasts
> Salt and pepper
> 3 teaspoons olive oil
> 2 cloves garlic, chopped or minced
> $\frac{1}{4}$ cup chopped shallots
> 10 to 12 imported olives
> 2 medium-size ripe tomatoes, chopped

Season the chicken breasts on both sides with salt and pepper. Heat 1 ½ teaspoons of olive oil over medium-high heat. Add the chicken and sear until well browned on both sides, about 3 minutes per side. Transfer the chicken to a plate and cover with foil.

Reduce heat to medium and add 1 ½ teaspoons of oil to the skillet. Add the garlic and shallots, and cook for a minute or two. Return the chicken breasts and juices to the skillet, add the olives and tomatoes, and simmer until the chicken is cooked through.

Linda Grant is the author of *Random Access Murder*, *Blind Trust* and *Vampire Bytes*.

Que Queen's Royal Rub
LOU JANE TEMPLE

$\mathcal{K}$ansas City's premier restaurateur Heaven Lee has a stash of secret sauces and rubs much enjoyed by her diners. Luckily, none has yet been responsible for any of the deaths that Heaven has become adept at solving.

¼ cup mixed peppercorns: black, white, and pink
¼ cups mustard seeds
¼ cup sesame seeds, lightly roasted
¼ cup kosher salt
1 dried ancho chili
¼ cup New Mexican ground red chilies
¼ cup brown sugar
1 tablespoon *each*: cinnamon, cumin, rubbed sage, cayenne, allspice,
    dried thyme, and tarragon

Combine the peppercorns, mustard seeds, sesame seeds, salt, and the ancho chili in the food processor and pulverize. Combine this mixture with all the other ingredients, taking care to mix carefully, as it will cause sneezing. Spread on baking sheets and toast in the oven lightly, about 10 minutes at 325 degrees. The toasting brings out the natural oils in the spices and develops the flavor more fully. Store in an airtight container in the freezer.

Use as a rub to season poultry, fish, or meat.

Lou Jane Temple writes culinary mysteries featuring Kansas City restaurateur, Heaven Lee, which include *Death by Rhubarb, Revenge of the Barbecue Queens* and *Bread on Arrival.*

Upper West Side Crock-Pot Chicken

(Or Simmered Pork Chops)

MARY BRINGLE

*Y*ou have no idea how many people will laugh themselves sick if my name appears in a *cook*book, but here goes. (This should be in a section called "Good Mystery Writers, Bad Cooks.")

In *Murder Most Gentrified*, freelance journalist Sarah Mason bemoans the fact that her once-colorful apartment house on Manhattan's Upper West Side has gone co-op and is losing its charm: *"In the past, the building had always held parties along more traditionally friendly lines—cocktails in one apartment, potluck dinner in another, and coffee and dessert in a third. Strange, now that they were a co-op, the spirit of cooperation had come to an end."* This dish is just the kind of thing Sarah—who also isn't much of a cook—would have brought to one of those lamented potlucks.

A delicious sauce in which to cook chicken (or simmer pork chops) can be made by using cream of mushroom soup as your base stock. Then you look for those leftover packets that come with Chinese takeout and add one packet of Chinese mustard, one of duck sauce, and one of soy sauce. Actually, Worcestershire sauce is better, but if you're out of it, the soy will do. You can also add a little sour cream in the chicken recipe, but I've always thought it was the condiments that did the trick. (With the pork chops, after you've browned them, it provides a way of cooking them on top of the stove without frying them. They don't dry out and get all stringy.) Kitchen wizardry!!

Mary Bringle has written four mysteries including *The Footpath Murder*, *Murder Most Gentrified* and *Little Creatures Everywhere*.

"Will you not sit down and share our roast duck with apple sauce and sage and onion stuffing?... Over a slice of the breast and a glass of the best any little differences may be adjusted."
—Lord Peter in Dorothy L. Sayer's *Busman's Honeymoon*

Hillary's Coq au Vin
PAULA CARTER

This recipe appears in *Leading an Elegant Death,* in which my protagonist, Jane Ferguson, who doesn't know how to cook, lands a job that, among other things, includes producing a cooking show for television for Hillary Scarborough. When Hillary asks Jane to come up with a recipe for coq au vin, it is a disaster, especially when the murderer accidentally tastes it. However, Hillary concocts the recipe, which saves the television show and possibly Jane's life.

Hillary's recipe makes an excellent and easy dish. She likes to serve it with a red Côtes du Rhône and thick slices of French bread fried in butter.

> 4 slices bacon, cut in small pieces
> 2 tablespoons chopped onion
> 2 ½ to 3 pounds broiler-fryer chicken, quartered
> 1 tablespoon flour
> 1 clove garlic, minced
> 1 bay leaf
> ½ teaspoon thyme
> 12 small white onions
> 1 cup sliced mushrooms
> ½ cup coarsely chopped carrots
> ¾ cup red wine (Hillary uses Burgundy)
> ½ cup clear chicken broth

In a large, heavy skillet, brown the bacon pieces and chopped onions. Remove the bacon bits. Add the chicken pieces and brown slowly in bacon drippings. Stir in the flour and cook until well-browned. Add the remaining ingredients. Heat to boiling and stir to loosen the crusty brown bits. Simmer for 45 minutes or until the meat is tender.

Serves 4 to 6.

Leading an Elegant Death is the first book in Paula Carter's series, *Murder by Design.*

Molly Brown's Incredibly Simple Chicken Cooked in Wine

MOLLY BROWN

*M*y favorite recipe is so simple it's embarrassing. It's also almost impossible to mess up, which is why anyone who gets invited to my house for dinner ends up with the same thing: my special chicken cooked in wine.

All you need is some chicken, an onion or two, some butter or margarine, and some wine.

The chicken needs to be cut into pieces. I'm lazy, so I just buy a pack of ready-cut breasts, or thighs, or drumsticks—whatever I'm in the mood for at the time. If I'm cooking breasts, one for each person is usually enough. For thighs, you should probably allow at least two per person, or three if the thighs are small.

Chop the onion roughly; you don't need little tiny pieces. Light a candle while you're chopping the onion and you won't cry.

Melt some butter or margarine in a frying pan, toss in the onion, then toss in the chicken. Cook it over a fairly high heat for a few minutes, turning the chicken so that it browns on both sides. Add a bit of salt and pepper if you like, and add more butter or margarine if necessary—you don't want the chicken to dry out. As soon as the chicken is nicely browned, pour the wine over it and turn the heat down to a gentle simmer.

The wine can be white, rosé, or red; it's up to you.

White wine gives the chicken a golden color and a lighter taste. Rosé gives it a pink color and a slightly fruity taste. Red gives the chicken a very deep color, almost purple, and has the strongest taste. (If in doubt, it's probably best to go for white or rosé; they seem to have the most general appeal.)

Be generous with the wine—use enough to completely cover the chicken—then let it condense down into a thick wine-and-onion sauce, which you will spoon over the chicken when you serve it. If the onions start to go black, don't worry. You can easily strain them out when it's time to serve the sauce, and burning the onions actually adds to the flavor. Just don't burn the chicken!

As soon as the chicken is cooked through, it's ready. The whole thing can be done in one frying pan in less than 15 minutes.

If I'm making a sit-down dinner, I'll usually serve the chicken with saffron rice and a selection of vegetables. If you want to jazz the main dish up a bit, you can throw some mushrooms into the pan, or maybe add a bit of garlic. (I have all kinds of tricks for jazzing up the side dishes as well, such as adding raisins or bits of red pepper to the rice, stirring a little bit of cream and parsley into the peas, glazing carrots with a touch of brown sugar, or stir-frying green beans with a couple of spoonfuls of Chinese yellow bean sauce. I've kept many vegetarians happy this way; those who don't want the chicken have still got plenty of things to eat.)

If I'm planning something more informal, drumsticks cooked this way work fine as cold finger snacks; I've even taken them on picnics. (With cold drumsticks, you don't want the sauce, so just put it to one side and freeze it until next time.)

When I had a party to celebrate the publication of my first book, I put out a big platter of cold skinless drumsticks that had been cooked in red wine. My guests' initial reaction was: "What *are* these purple things?" But their second reaction was: "How do you make them?" and the third was: "Are there any more?"

Molly Brown is author of *Cracker: To Say I Love You*, a novelization based on the British television series and *Invitation to a Funeral*, a humorous historical whodunit set in Restoration London.

Ray Donne's Barbecued Chicken

WILLIAM RELLING, JR.

*H*aving grown up in St. Louis, Missouri (a hotbed of great grilling), I've fond memories of a place called the Academy Bar-B-Q, sadly no longer in business, I'm told. The Academy wasn't much patronized by folks of WASP-y persuasion like me, but my friends and I loved it. Our usual order was: "Gimme a slab of ribs and a 7-ounce Miller's!" Miller High-Life, that is. A perfect beverage-and-food combination.

I've never told anyone this, but one of the reasons why I moved to southern California some two decades ago is because you can barbecue year-round. My wife, Ann, jokingly calls me "The Q-King of Pasadena," a title I wear as humbly as I can. I hope one day to pass on the crown to my son, Tom.

As, I imagine, Ray Donne will one day pass on his crown to his son, Jack, the hero in my books. Right now, though, Ray's still champ.

The following simple recipe is a little more yuppified than down-home, but it's still tasty. I suggest a crisp Semillon or a spicy Gewürztraminer for an accompanying beverage, though cold beer would work too. The wine shouldn't be too chilled, say around 60 degrees. Steamed fresh vegetables, a little basmati or wild rice on the side—hey, you're there!

¼ cup olive oil
¼ cup apple juice
2 tablespoons Worcestershire sauce
Juice of 1 lemon
2 cloves garlic, finely chopped
1 frying chicken, cut into pieces

Using a whisk, mix the ingredients (except for the chicken) to make a marinade. Put the marinade in a bowl and add the chicken, making sure all the pieces can soak. Cover the bowl and let it sit, refrigerated, for at least 6 hours.

Fire up the Q, get the coals medium-hot, and grill the chicken. Cook it as slowly as possible, turning frequently so it doesn't burn. The meat is done when you can pierce it and the juices run clear. Don't overcook, unless you like your chicken charred.

William Relling, Jr.'s hero Jack Donne appears in *Deadly Vintage* and *Sweet Poison*.

Herb of Death Dressing

In Agatha Christie's Miss Marple story "The Herb of Death," Sylvia Keene dies after dining on roast duck stuffed with sage dressing. It seems poisonous foxglove leaves have mistakenly been picked along with the sage. It's a terrible accident. Or is it?

We've adapted this time-honored family recipe for those who wish to stuff their duck (or turkey or goose) with a classic sage dressing à la Christie. But watch out for that foxglove!

    1-pound loaf of white bread, cubed and dried
    4 tablespoons butter or margarine
    1 cup chopped celery (4 ribs)
    1 medium onion, chopped
    2 tablespoons minced fresh parsley
    2 tablespoons chopped fresh sage leaves
    1 teaspoon salt
    1 cup chicken broth

The day before: Cut the bread into ½-inch cubes and allow to dry overnight on a cookie sheet.

The day of your dinner: Preheat the oven to 375 degrees. In a skillet, melt the butter over a low flame. Add the celery, onion, parsley, sage, and salt, and simmer until the vegetables and herbs are soft. Add the chicken broth and bring to a boil. Place the bread crumbs in a bowl, and pour the mixture over them. Stir with a large fork until mixed. If the stuffing appears dry, add a little boiling water.

Transfer the mixture to a covered casserole dish and bake for 30 minutes. Or, if cooking in the poultry, refrigerate the unbaked mixture and, when cool, stuff the cavity of the bird immediately before placing it in the oven.

Turkey Potpie

JEANNE M. DAMS

This is the potpie that widow Dorothy Martin made for widower Chief Constable Alan Nesbit when he came over for supper, a discussion of murder, and perhaps a little dalliance!

4 carrots
1 cup frozen hash-brown potatoes
Salt
Water
1 cup frozen peas
4 ribs celery, chopped
1 large onion, chopped
8 tablespoons butter, divided
6 tablespoons flour

1 chicken bouillon cube
2 cups milk
1/4 pound processed American cheese, cubed
3 cups of leftover roast turkey, cubed
　(use all white meat or a combination
　of white and dark)
1 4-ounce can mushrooms
Pastry for a 2-crust pie

Cook the carrots and potatoes until tender in boiling salted water to cover; stir in the frozen peas and bring to a boil again. Remove from heat and drain.

Meanwhile, sauté the celery and onion in 2 tablespoons of butter till limp but not brown.

In a large saucepan or skillet, melt 6 tablespoons butter, stir in the flour, and cook to a roux. Preheat the oven to 425 degrees. Dissolve the bouillon cube in 1/2 cup boiling water; gradually add with milk to the flour roux. Cook slowly, stirring constantly with a whisk, until thick and smooth. Stir in the cheese, turkey, mushrooms, and vegetables. Pat the bottom crust into a deep-dish pie plate or casserole. Spoon in the turkey mixture. Lay the top crust over, seal the edges, and slash with a knife to make slits for steam to escape. Bake at 425 degrees for 20 minutes, and then at 350 degrees for another 30 minutes. Serve hot.

This is a wonderful way to use up leftover turkey, or it could be made with chunks of chicken breast. Don't try to improve the cheese; wonderful cheddar will give it the wrong texture. I use Pillsbury refrigerated pie crust for this and most of my pies; it's quick and easy and consistent, which is more than I can say for my homemade version! For this recipe the bottom crust, at least, will have to be rolled out to a bigger circle. The only problem with this recipe is that it doesn't reheat well, so if you have a small family, make it in two smaller pans and freeze one for baking later, or serve when company's coming.

Makes 6 to 8 servings.

Jeanne M. Dams is the author of *Trouble in the Town Hall, Malice in Miniature* and *Holy Terror in the Hebrides*, all of which feature Dorothy Martin.

April Woo's Crispy Hacked Duck
LESLIE GLASS

April Woo, a detective sergeant in the NYPD, is the first Asian law-enforcement officer in American crime fiction. She also happens to be the daughter of a Chinese chef. April learned to cook from her father, and he never gave her more than a list of ingredients and the methods for cooking—roast, stir fry, deep fry, dry fry, steam, twice cook, etc. When April asked how much of each ingredient she should use, Chef Woo always told his daughter, "Up to you." When she asked how long she should cook each item, his reply was, "Until done." With this sly encouragement to experiment and find her own standard for "taste good," April became a first-class cook.

The first meal she cooks for her boyfriend, Mike Sanchez, includes roast hacked duck.

1 fresh duck, washed and patted dried	1 tablespoon honey
A thumb-size piece of fresh ginger	Five-spice powder, to taste
2 scallions, chopped	3 tablespoons hoisin sauce
¼ cup ketchup	Pinch of white pepper
3 tablespoons dark soy sauce	

Cut off the neck and first joint of the wing tips of the duck. Hack off the extra flaps of skin and stab the duck all over with a fork.

Peel and slice the ginger. Insert half of the ginger and the scallions in the duck cavity. Reserve the rest of the ginger for the marinade. Place the duck in an ovenproof baking dish.

Mix the ketchup, remaining ginger, soy sauce, honey, five-spice powder, hoisin sauce, and pepper. Mix well and then knead it into the duck (or chicken or squab or spareribs). Marinate for 6 hours or overnight.

Preheat the oven to 350 degrees. Roast until crispy and brown—for a duck, about an hour and a half.

Remove the duck from the oven and let stand until cool enough to handle, then hack the meat from the bones with a sharp knife or a cleaver. Serve the hacked duck meat on a bed of shredded lettuce with pickled vegetables, and extra hoisin sauce on the side.

Note: The Chinese love pickles, and they are easily made. Slice (or julienne) and salt to taste one crunchy raw vegetable, or any combination of cucumbers, colorful peppers, radishes, shredded red cabbage, daikon. Bathe salted veggies in rice vinegar with a dash of sugar for several hours.

April Woo, the hero created by Leslie Glass, has appeared in *Burning Time*, *Hanging Time*, *Loving Time* and *Stealing Time*.

SECRET MEAT-INGS

Steamed Pork with Pickled Cabbage
LISA SEE

One of my favorite childhood dishes was this steamed pork with pickled vegetable. My grandfather made a delicious version, but there was also a place in Chinatown—I never knew the name, we just called it "the little place"—where we would go at least once a week to have it. The Chinese name for the pickled vegetable is *dung choy*, but we simply call it "that *choy*." As in: "you know that *choy*?" or "I just picked up five jars of that *choy*."

My main character, Liu Hulan, inspector with Beijing's Ministry of Public Security, would also be enamored of this dish for its surface simplicity (she's a busy woman and this takes about five minutes to put together), its fragrance (it's so pungent that if you order it in a Chinese restaurant, the waiter's apt to say, "Oh, you're an American. You won't like it."), and its taste (which is tangy and thoroughly evocative of China).

1 pound ground pork	2 teaspoons dry sherry
1 can water chestnuts, peeled and coarsely chopped	1 teaspoon sugar
	2 teaspoons Asian sesame oil
3 green onions, chopped (include the green!)	1 teaspoon pepper
1 tablespoon soy sauce	Couple tablespoons Tianjin preserved vegetable (pickled cabbage)

Mix the first 8 ingredients together. Mush it down flat onto a heatproof plate. Take a couple of tablespoons of the preserved vegetable and spread it over the top.

Set up a steamer dish that's deep enough and wide enough to hold the plate. (You can always use a wok and lid.) Fill with a couple of inches of water and bring to a boil. Set the plate on the rack, cover, lower heat to simmer, and steam for 20 minutes or until the pork is done.

Serve with rice and some sautéed spinach.

Note 1: Don't pour off the water that's accumulated on the plate during steaming. That's now a wonderful sauce that will taste great on your rice.

Note 2: Tianjin preserved vegetable comes in a lovely earthenware jar, from which you'll get many dishes. (Don't worry. This stuff is *seriously* preserved and meant to withstand the years of deep cold and blistering heat typical of the Chinese countryside, so you can keep it forever.) When it's empty, the jar makes a neat vase or pencil holder.

Note 3: The first 8 ingredients can also serve as the base for 3 other dishes. Pork with pickled turnip, pork with salted duck eggs, and pork with salted fish. Pickled turnip (available in Chinese groceries) comes in a small can, so use the whole thing. You can also get salted duck eggs in Chinese groceries. Just peel them, discard the egg white, crumble the yolk, and sprinkle over the top of the pork. There are 2 varieties of salted fish. One comes in a jar of oil. Simply drain and chop the fish. If you use salted dried fish, soak it in warm water for 20 minutes, drain, and chop. Use about 6 tablespoons sprinkled on top of the pork mixture. With all of these recipes, steam for 20 minutes or until the pork is done.

Lisa See's first mystery novel, set in Beijing and Los Angeles and featuring Liu Hulan, is *Flower Net*.

Pork Saté

PHILIP R. CRAIG

$\mathcal{M}$y protagonist, J.W. Jackson, loves to cook (as do I) and neither of us has any qualms about sharing our recipes. Here's a favorite J.W. enjoys while having a casual meal on his porch in Martha's Vineyard.

  1 ½ pounds pork tenderloin (can also be made with chicken breasts
      instead of pork)
  ¼ cup butter
  1 tablespoon lemon juice
  Grated lemon rind from 1 lemon
  ½ teaspoon Tabasco sauce
  3 tablespoons grated onion
  3 tablespoons light brown sugar
  1 teaspoon coriander
  ½ teaspoon ground cumin
  ¼ teaspoon ground ginger
  1 clove garlic, crushed
  ½ cup Indonesian soya sauce or Kikkoman teriyaki sauce
  Salt and pepper to taste (go easy on salt)

Cut the pork tenderloin into ¾-inch cubes and place in a shallow glass dish. Melt the butter in a saucepan and add the remaining ingredients. Bring to a boil and simmer 5 minutes. Pour over the meat, cover, and leave overnight in refrigerator. Turn the meat periodically.

Remove the meat from the marinade (reserve), and put 5 or 6 pieces on a skewer. Grill on a barbecue for 15 minutes until done, turning frequently (don't overcook). The meat may also be cooked in a broiler. Reheat the marinade and pour over the meat. Set the skewers on a platter in a bed of rice. Good served with a peanut dipping sauce. Serve with a spinach salad.

Serves 6 to 8 and may also be used as an appetizer.

Philip R. Craig's Martha's Vineyard mystery series includes *A Beautiful Place to Die, Death on a Vineyard Beach* and *A Deadly Vineyard Holiday.*

Pork Chops Black Mariah

JOHN DANDOLA

*T*he male lead of my *Dead at the Box Office* and its sequel, *Dead in Their Sights*, is based on my grandfather. That choice seemed more obvious than unique because the plot of *Dead at the Box Office* revolves around the world premiere of MGM's *Edison the Man* in my hometown during 1940, and my grandfather had served as a personal messenger boy to Thomas Alva Edison during the 1910s. Cultivated yet rough 'n' tumble whenever he had to be, my grandfather was just that sort of figure to whom the locals turned whenever there was trouble. A murder mystery seemed the perfect setting for him. He was one of my heroes and he died when I was ten.

"Why," you might ask, "would MGM unveil a major motion picture in a small New Jersey town?" Because it is the town where Edison had lived and worked since 1886 and where he died in 1931. It is also the unlikely site of the world's first motion picture studio. That studio—a replica of which still stands on display—was little more than a tarpapered shack nicknamed "black Mariah" because it so resembled the horse-drawn police paddy wagons similarly dubbed.

While I was writing *Dead in Their Sights*, my wife, Patricia, (who shares both her birthday and her culinary skills with my grandmother), surprised me by updating one of my grandfather's favorite dishes and christening it Pork Chops Black Mariah.

> 6 to 8 pork chops
> Oil (to coat bottom of pan)
> Fresh garlic
> 2 stalks celery, diced
> 2 medium onions, sliced
> 1 cup Marsala wine
> ½ cup water
> 2 beef bouillon cubes
> 6 carrots, peeled and quartered
> Bisto (a starch-based mix for browning, seasoning, and thickening gravy)

Brown the pork chops in oil; remove from pan.

Sauté the garlic, celery, and onions together in the same pan; cover and cook for 2 minutes; remove from the pan.

Add 1 cup of Marsala wine to the pan; put the pork chops back in the pan; add water and bouillon cubes; put the celery and onions on top of the pork chops; add carrots; cover and simmer for 20 minutes. Mix the Bisto in cold water; stir; add to the pan to thicken the gravy and serve.

Serves 6 to 8.

John Dandola's other books include *Wind of Time* and *Wicked is the Wind*.

Hangtown Fry

PENNY WARNER

According to California legend, the unique dish called Hangtown Fry was created during the Gold Rush of 1849. When a dirt-covered miner from Shirttail Bend arrived at the Cary House in Hangtown (now Placerville) with a handful of gold nuggets, he demanded the most expensive meal on the menu. When told it would be either oysters or eggs, he asked the cook to mix them together and serve up the dish. It's been a popular request at the cafés and diners along the California Mother Lode's gold chain for nearly a 150 years, but Connor Westphal prefers them at The Nugget Café in Flat Skunk.

> ½ pound bacon
> 2 tablespoons butter or margarine
> 12 medium oysters
> Flour for dredging
> 1 egg, lightly beaten, for dipping
> 1 cup bread or cracker crumbs
> 6 eggs, lightly beaten
> ¼ cup cream or milk
> ¼ cup grated Parmesan cheese
> Salt and pepper to taste

Fry the bacon in a large skillet until crisp. Remove, drain, and crumble into medium pieces. Pour the bacon fat from the skillet and add the butter. Dip each oyster in flour, egg, and bread crumbs, and fry over medium heat until golden brown, about 1 minute per side. Beat the 6 eggs with the milk and Parmesan cheese. Pour over the oysters, stir, and cook until set. Add salt and pepper to taste, top with the bacon, and serve immediately.

Penny Warner's series featuring news reporter Connor Westphal includes *Dead Body Language* and *Right to Remain Silent*.

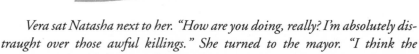

Vera sat Natasha next to her. "How are you doing, really? I'm absolutely distraught over those awful killings." She turned to the mayor. "I think the committee should issue a public statement of outrage that someone is killing American chefs."

The mayor sneered. "Actually, I'm not certain it is even against the law....Certainly it is not against French law."

—Nan and Ivan Lyons, *Someone is Killing the Great Chefs of America*

Red Beans and Rice

SARAH SHANKMAN

*S*am (Samantha) Adams has always been handy with a knife and fork, growing up at the knee of Peaches Johnson, one of Atlanta's finest cooks. Then she was lucky enough to live in northern California, which enjoys a bounty of great produce and fabulous chefs of all ethnicities. But for the past few years Sam's been living in Covington, Louisiana, on the north shore of Lake Pontchatrain, close but not too close to her boyfriend, Harry Zack. Harry, who was raised in New Orleans' Garden District, considers red beans and rice a staple of life. Sam and Harry both cook, but their favorite version of this earthy dish is that prepared by their great friend/chef/and Harry's partner in the BBQ business, Lavert Washington. While most visitors to New Orleans enjoy more exotic fare such as oysters Rockefeller and pompano papillote, it is this kind of home cooking that gives New Orleans its true down-home flavor.

Red beans and rice is a favorite "comfort food" of New Orleans. It's traditionally served on Monday, even to this day, because Monday was wash day, when the beans and ham bone could simmer all day while the wash was being done. If the weekend's indulgences have been too much, red beans and rice for Monday lunch is a time-honored hangover cure.

> 1 ½ cups (12 ounces) dried kidney beans, rinsed
> 1 ham hock or meaty ham bone (optional)
> ¾ teaspoon salt
> 1 tablespoon vegetable oil
> 12 ounces andouille or other spicy smoked sausage such as kielbasa,
>   cut into ½-inch slices
> 1 large onion, chopped
> 1 medium green bell pepper, seeded and chopped
> 1 stalk celery, chopped
> 4 green onions, thinly sliced (both white and green parts)
> 2 bay leaves
> ¼ teaspoon freshly ground black pepper
> ½ teaspoon dried thyme
> ½ teaspoon dried oregano
> 1 teaspoon garlic powder
> ½ teaspoon cayenne pepper (or to taste)
> ½ teaspoon hot-pepper sauce such as Tabasco (or to taste)
> 3 cups water
> 1 ½ cups long-grain rice
> ½ teaspoon salt

In a large heavy-bottomed pot, cover the beans in cold water and soak overnight or for 8 hours. To quick-soak, bring the water and beans to a boil, uncovered, for 2 minutes. Remove from heat, cover, and let stand for 1 hour. Drain the beans, rinse the pan, and return the beans to the pan. Cover the beans with 6 cups of fresh cold water. Add the ham hock or bone, if desired. Bring to a simmer over medium-high heat, reduce to low, and cook, covered, for 1 to 1 ½ hours, or until the beans are almost tender, stirring occasionally. Add salt.

Remove the ham hock with tongs, cut any meat off the bone, and return the meat, but not the bone, to the pot.

In a large skillet, heat the oil, add the sausage, and cook, stirring for 5 minutes or until it begins to brown. Add the onion, bell pepper, celery, and green onions and cook, stirring, 5 minutes, or until the vegetables begin to soften. Add the sausage-vegetable mix to the beans. Add the bay leaves, black pepper, thyme, oregano, garlic, and cayenne and continue cooking, uncovered, over low heat, for 30 to 45 minutes or until beans are very tender. If the beans should begin to scorch, remove immediately from heat. Do not stir. Change the beans to another pot without scraping in any burned beans.

Meanwhile, prepare the rice. In a medium-size pot, bring the water to a boil, add the rice and salt, and simmer, covered, 20 minutes or until tender and the liquid is absorbed.

Using the back of a large spoon, mash about $\frac{1}{4}$ of the beans against the side of the pan and stir to thicken the bean mixture. Season to taste with hot-pepper sauce. Adjust all the seasonings to taste.

To serve, divide the rice among 6 shallow bowls or plates and ladle the beans over the rice. Pass the hot sauce. Serve with a salad with zesty Italian dressing and hot French bread.

Sarah Shankman's Samantha Adams series includes *First Kill All the Lawyers, Then Hang All Liars* and *Now Let's Talk of Graves*.

Triggerman's Rattlesnake

T. JEFFERSON PARKER

I picked this simple, delicious, and offbeat dish because my heroine serves it to an unsuspecting fellow in my novel, *The Triggerman's Dance*. The poor guy can't decide if it's fish or chicken.

> 1 rattlesnake
> ½ cube butter
> 1 tablespoon chopped garlic
> 3 tablespoons chopped green onion
> 1 tablespoon chopped ginger

Kill, skin, and dress a rattlesnake. Remove the head because a dead snake can still clamp his mouth on you. Cut into 1-inch sections. Rinse well.

In a heavy skillet, sauté the butter with the spices over a medium flame. Arrange the rattlesnake pieces, not touching each other, and cover. Cook 5 minutes, turn the sections, cover again. Cook 5 more minutes.

Salt and pepper lightly.

Serve with a robust red wine, such as the Bogle 1996 Petite Sirah, and enjoy!

Number of servings depends on length of the snake.

T. Jefferson Parker's crime novels include *Laguna Heat*, *Little Saigon* and *The Blue Hour*.

Karai Lamb

GRAHAM THOMAS

$\mathcal{M}$y series character, Detective Chief Superintendent Erskine Powell of New Scotland Yard, is an unrepentant curryholic. In *Malice in Cornwall* he orders this dish at his favorite Indian Restaurant, K2 Tandoori in London. Now you can enjoy it too.

The *karai* method of cooking, named for the round-bottomed pan (similar to a wok), originated in Pakistan. It inspired the Balti style of cooking that is so popular in Britain nowadays. The beauty of the method is that it is so easy. Although the ingredients are similar to those one might use in Chinese stir-fry, the result is deliciously different.

> 4 tablespoons cooking oil (any vegetable oil except olive oil will do)
> 1 tablespoon fresh garlic, very finely chopped
> 2 tablespoons fresh ginger, peeled and very finely chopped
> 1 pound boned fresh leg of lamb, cut into 1-inch cubes
> 1 medium onion, sliced
> ½ cup canned crushed tomatoes
> ½ teaspoon hot red chili powder or cayenne
>   (use more or less, depending on your tolerance to heat)
> 1 teaspoon paprika
> ½ teaspoon salt (or to taste)
> ½ green bell pepper, coarsely chopped into 1-inch pieces
> Green onions, finely chopped for garnish

Heat the oil in a well-seasoned wok or large cast-iron or non-stick pan over high heat. Add the garlic and ginger and stir-fry for 30 seconds. Add everything else except the green pepper and green onions and mix well. The secret of the *karai* method is to cook the ingredients quickly over fairly high heat, *stirring almost continuously* to prevent burning. If necessary, turn the heat down slightly or add a tablespoon of water to keep the contents from sticking to the pan. The lamb should take about 20 minutes to cook. Add the green pepper during the last 5 minutes. Garnish with the chopped green onion.

Serve immediately with basmati rice or Indian bread (pita will do in a pinch), a tossed green salad, and, if you're so inclined, a chilled lager to put out the fire.

Serves 4.

Detective Chief Superintendent Erskine Powell appears in Graham Thomas' *Malice in Cornwall* and *Malice in the Highlands*.

Lamb Stew

JEROME DOOLITTLE

The hero of my Tom Bethany series lives alone in an apartment in Cambridge, Massachusetts. He mainly eats stew, which he makes on Sundays and freezes. I used to do the same thing when I lived alone in a Cambridge apartment. My favorite, and therefore his:

Dump 3 pounds of lamb, bones and all, into a pot with a teaspoon of peppercorns and 9 cups of water. Neck bones are best, but shank or breast will do. Bring to a boil, cover, and simmer. Don't bother to skim the scum unless you're the kind of person who won't eat a piece of candy after it's fallen on the floor. In fact, if you're that kind of a person, forget this whole recipe. And get a life.

Once the meat has simmered for 1 ½ hours, fish it out and set it aside in a bowl to cool. Remove the fat from the broth, or don't. Whatever. Whack up 2 carrots and 3 onions. Scrape the carrots first if you feel like it, but the fact is, we're about to sterilize them anyway. Better peel the onions, though, because the papery stuff gets in your teeth. Toss it all in the pot, add a cup of uncooked barley, and start simmering again. Keep going till the onions have pretty much disappeared, the carrots are soft, and the barley is too. Now pick the meat off the bones and toss it back in, minus fat.

Chop up one of those 10- or 12-ounce boxes of mushrooms, using the same cleaning standards you applied to the carrots, only remembering this time that mushrooms grow in horse manure. Toss in the mushrooms, along with as much thyme, cumin, chopped garlic, and ground pepper as you want. Cook just long enough for the mushrooms to soften up, then add a ½ stick of butter and 1 cup of cream. Once the butter melts, you're done. It may look a little soupy, but it will thicken up as it cools.

For immediate eating, rip a hole in one corner of a bag of frozen peas and pour a handful of them into your bowl. Close up the bag with a twist-tie and put it back in the freezer. Now ladle lots of stew on top of the peas, stir, and eat. Trust me on this business with the peas. Just do it the way I say.

Once the remaining stew has cooled, portion it out into beautifully designed and incredibly expensive refrigerator containers from Williams-Sonoma or into old yogurt cups. Up to you, but Tom Bethany uses the pint-size containers that Stoneyfield yogurt comes in. They hold up under repeated microwaving.

This recipe has no salt, because both Tom and I are both health-and-fitness fanatics who regard our bodies as temples. The rest of you may salt to taste.

Jerome Doolittle is the author of *Head Lock*, *Bear Hug*, and *Half Nelson*.

Deep-Dish Lamb Pie

LEV RAPHAEL

*T*his meal appears at a dark time in my third Nick Hoffman mystery *The Death of a Constant Lover*. Nick, a tenure-seeking assistant professor at the State University of Michigan in Michiganapolis, is disturbed by the unsolved murder of one of his student. The killing may be due to a growing climate of intolerance on his bucolic Midwestern campus, pitting all sorts of people—including the increasingly polarized faculty—against each other. The whole mess has left Nick, whose tenure prospects are doubtful, wondering if he'd even want to stay if he *were* to get tenure. As if that isn't enough uncertainty, his partner Stefan, SUM's writer-in-residence, has been left stunned and brooding by bad news from his publisher. So Nick's surprised to come home from campus one afternoon to find Stefan preparing this complex meal by himself. Not only have the two of them always cooked it together, Stefan's been so depressed he's seemed beyond making toast. But Stefan is unexpectedly ebullient now and every surface in the kitchen is covered. So what if his career's going down in flames, he says, at least they can have a terrific meal. Nick suspects this jauntiness has clearly been helped along by a few drinks, but he, too, is willing to forget their troubles with good wine and good food—for that night, anyway. So he joins Stefan in preparation and forgetting.

I haven't had as exciting and murder-filled life as Nick has, but I have made this pie and it's superb. While it takes a lot of prep time, it's certainly worth the effort. Try it with a Gigondas or Châteuneuf-du-Pape.

> 3 medium potatoes, peeled and diced
> 2 ½ cups low-fat milk
> 1 small celery root, trimmed, peeled, and diced
> 2 teaspoons salt
> 1 teaspoon freshly ground pepper
> 1 teaspoon olive oil
> 1 onion, peeled and minced
> 2 cloves garlic, peeled and minced
> 1 pound ground lamb
> 1 teaspoon ground cumin
> ½ teaspoon ground ginger
> ½ teaspoon ground cinnamon
> ¼ teaspoon cayenne pepper
> ½ teaspoon saffron threads
> 1 tablespoon grated lemon rind
> ¼ cup minced dried apricots
> ¼ cup slivered almonds
> 1 acorn or butternut squash, peeled and diced
> ¾ cup low-sodium chicken broth
> 3 tablespoons minced coriander leaves

Place the potatoes and milk in a saucepan. Simmer slowly, about 6 minutes. Add the celery root. Simmer until tender, about 6 minutes. Drain, reserving the milk. Pass the potatoes and celery root through a food mill. Stir in ½ cup of the reserved milk, 1 teaspoon salt, and the pepper. Set aside.

Heat the olive oil in a large nonstick skillet over medium-low heat. Add the onion and garlic, and cook until soft, about 7 minutes. Add the lamb, add the spices. Increase the heat to medium-high. Cook, stirring frequently, until lightly browned. Stir in the remaining ingredients, including the reserved milk and remaining salt. Increase the heat to high. Simmer 5 minutes.

Place the lamb mixture in a 10-inch quiche dish. Spread the potato puree evenly over the top. Cover with foil. Bake 1 hour at 350 degrees.

Preheat the broiler. Place the dish under the broiler until the top is brown.

Makes 6 servings.

Food-loving Nick Hoffman also appears in Lev Raphael's *Let's Get Criminal* and *The Edith Wharton Murders*.

Sauce Sauvage à la Claudine

DANA STABENOW

*S*studied French one summer at the Sorbonne, and several of the other students decided they wanted to take a cooking class. They needed one more student to make it fly and browbeat me into going along, although my sole skill in the kitchen to that date was tuna fish sandwiches (FYI, I use gherkins, not dills).

The chef was Mme. Claudine Loez, who looked as if she had just stepped out of *The Arabian Nights* and who cooked like she'd taught Julia Child how. She had a kitchen big enough for one goat and a stove the size of a postage stamp, and there she began to instruct us in the mysteries of "la belle cuisine."

She designed the course around the fresh foods native to each student's home, and when she heard I was from Alaska her eyes lit up. "Quelle sauvage," she breathed, and on the spot made up right out of her head the following sauce, also known as a roux, for wild-game meats. I've used it on caribou and moose to (ahem) tremendous acclaim, and when the freezer is empty it's not bad on lean roast beef, either.

So here goes:

> 1 cup dry white wine
> 7 tablespoons raspberry vinegar
> Salt and pepper to taste
> ½ bunch green onions, minced
> 2 heaping tablespoons sugar
> 1 stick of butter

Pour the wine into a saucepan, add the vinegar, salt, pepper, onions, and sugar. Bring to a slow boil, reduce heat, and cook down to a few tablespoons of liquid. Add the butter 1 pat at a time, constantly stirring. Serve over wild-game roast or the leanest roast beef you can find. Yum.

Dana Stabenow is the author of the Kate Shugak mystery series which includes *Break Up, Blood Will Tell*, and *A Cold-Blooded Business*.

Detroit Stuffed Peppers à la Amos Walker

LOREN D. ESTLEMAN

This particular dish is dear to my heart. My mother, a first-generation American of Romany Gypsy stock, brought me up in rural Michigan on stuffed peppers, and this was the first challenging dish I assayed during my first marriage. I used every pot and pan in the house to make two peppers, and when it turned out successful, I realized that there was no recipe I couldn't conquer; a cook was born. The skills I acquired subsequently helped me to survive my divorce and have done much to balance the domestic responsibilities during my second marriage, similar to the way the character of Amos Walker has blessed my career. It seemed right and proper that I should name the recipe after him.

> 4 medium-size green peppers
> 2 pounds ground sirloin
> 1 15-ounce can tomato sauce
> 1 cup long-grain rice
> 1 cup diced onions
> ½ cup red wine
> ½ cup sour cream
> 1 tablespoon oregano

Slice the tops off the peppers (save them), remove the seeds, and parboil the peppers and tops for 3 minutes. Brown the sirloin in a skillet. Cook the rice. Combine the sirloin, rice, tomato sauce, onion, red wine, sour cream, and oregano. Spoon the mixture into the peppers. Replace the tops on the peppers and place in a casserole dish, spooning the excess mixture into the spaces between. Cover and bake at 350 degrees for 45 minutes. Let stand covered for 5 minutes before serving.

Loren D. Estleman's Amos Walker appears in *Never Street* and *Sugartown*.

> *She watched as Mabel scoured the carving knife. Mitchell Pierce had been killed with a hunting knife. Carving knives. Hunting knives. It suddenly seemed that there were an awful lot of knives in the news on Sanpere.*
> —Katherine Hall Page, *The Body in the Basement*

Harry James Denton's Killer Jack Daniel's Marinade

STEVEN WOMACK

As a member of the Tennessee Squire Association and owner of one square inch of land in Lynchburg, Tennessee, home of the Jack Daniel's distillery, I share this killer marinade. Its taste is due to the unique flavor of Jack Daniel's Tennessee Sour Mash (never call it bourbon), which brings out the best in just about anything that's barbecued or grilled. This recipe makes plenty of marinade for at least a pound of beef, chicken, pork (especially tenderloin), or seafood (especially shrimp).

> 1 tablespoon whole black peppercorns
> ½ cup olive oil
> ¼ cup maple syrup
> ¼ cup Jack Daniel's Tennessee Sour Mash Whiskey
> 2 tablespoons Lea & Perrins Worcestershire Sauce
> 1 teaspoon Liquid Smoke
> ½ teaspoon fresh thyme

Beat the whole black peppers into submission, and mix with the other ingredients. The longer you marinade, the better. Go for at least 4 hours with anything but seafood. For seafood, 1 hour max. Adjust portions for larger parties, and enjoy!

Dead Folks' Blues, the first in Steven Womack's series featuring bumbling newspaperman-turned-PI Harry James Denton, from "Music City, U.S.A." won the Edgar as Best Original Paperback Novel. Others in the series include *Way Past Dead*, *Murder Manual* and *Dirty Money*.

Saturday Night Special

LOUISE HENDRICKSEN

My character, Dr. Amy Prescott, is a better forensic scientist than a cook, so she collects recipes that require little preparation. When she wants to impress her guests she whips together what she calls "The Saturday Night Special." It's quick, it tingles the taste buds, it looks spectacular, and men love it. Make a green salad, light the candles, and enjoy the compliments.

1 pound lean ground meat
    (beef, turkey, or ground Italian sausages—casings removed)
1 large onion, chopped
1 green pepper, chopped
1 clove garlic, minced
1 15-ounce jar marinara or spaghetti sauce
¾ teaspoon Italian seasoning or ¼ teaspoon *each*: dry basil, oregano,
    and thyme leaves
1 cup cheddar or Jack cheese
1 cup mozzarella cheese
2 eggs
1 cup milk
1 cup all-purpose flour
½ teaspoon salt
1 tablespoon oil
3 tablespoons grated Parmesan cheese.

Brown the ground meat over medium-high heat until crumbly. Drain off all the fat except 2 tablespoons. Add the onion, pepper, and garlic; sauté until limp. Drain off the fat again, then add the spaghetti sauce and Italian seasoning; let simmer uncovered for 5 minutes.

Spread the meat mixture in the bottom of a 9-by-13-inch baking dish. Sprinkle the cheddar and mozzarella cheese evenly over the meat.

In a blender container, whirl together the eggs, milk, flour, salt, and 1 tablespoon of cooking oil until smooth. Pour over the meat and cheese mixture. Sprinkle the top with Parmesan cheese. Bake in a 400-degree oven until puffy and browned, about 30 minutes.

Makes 4 to 6 servings.

Louise Hendricksen's Dr. Amy Prescott appears in *Lethal Legacy*.

Potato Chulent—"Yaptzok"

ROCHELLE MAJER KRICH

A traditional Sabbath lunch in Jewish homes includes a casserole-type dish called a "chulent" (the *ch* pronounced as in *chuck*), which is prepared Friday afternoon and simmered in the oven or in a Crock-Pot until it is served, piping hot, the next day. A chulent typically consists of potatoes, meat, and a variety of beans and seasonings. A beanless grated-potato version called "yaptzok" (I'm guessing at the spelling) originated in Poland for consumption during Passover, when legumes aren't permitted.

Yaptzok isn't limited to Passover. It was a year-long favorite in my home when I was growing up. Sabbath mornings I'd wake up to the tantalizing aroma of meat and onion and potato, and hours before lunch I'd savor in my mind the steaming hot, delectable, glutinous mounds of potato, the chunks of browned, crunchy crust. When I married, I learned the recipe from my mother, who learned it from her mother as a young girl in Poland. My husband and our children and their spouses love yaptzok, and it has become a popular offering at Sabbath after-services celebrations and a test of the caterer's mettle. ("Sure he makes a good bean chulent. But can he make a *yaptzok*?")

Here's my mother's recipe:

> 1 medium onion, grated
> 5 pounds potatoes (15 to 20), peeled and grated
> 2 eggs
> ½ cup oil
> ½ cup water
> Salt and pepper to taste
> 1 pound or more of flanken, chuck, short rib, or stew meat

When I was a teenager, my mother and I would share grating the potatoes and onion on a flat, webbed metal grater that I still have. I remember teary eyes (the onion) and scraped knuckles—mine; my mother was an expert grater. That was years ago, before the food processor arrived. Some of my friends still insist on hand-grating. I use a processor. To me, the yaptzok tastes the same, and my knuckles are spared.

Grate the onion first (*yes*, in the processor; no one will know). Shred half the potatoes; grate the other half on FINE. Mix the potatoes with the onion quickly to keep them from turning black. Add the eggs, oil, water, salt, and pepper. Cube the meat and set it aside.

You'll need a heavy pot—5 quarts or larger. Cast iron is good if you have it, or enameled steel. Coat the bottom and sides of the pot with oil, and heat the pot on the stove top. When the oil is hot (drop in a tiny bit of the potato mixture—if it sizzles, it's ready), pour half the potato mixture into the pot, being careful to avoid any splattering oil. Add all the meat. Pour the remainder of the potato mixture on top of the meat.

Bake, uncovered, at 350 degrees for 30 minutes. Remove the pot; stir in about a cup of water. (Sorry, the exact measurement you'll learn by trial and error, as I did.) Cover the pot and return it to the oven, reducing the temperature to 225 degrees. Leave the yaptzok in the oven until lunch the next day.

(If you like a looser yaptzok, add more water; if you like a thicker one, add less. But add too little water and you'll have only crust. Which isn't necessarily a bad thing. It's what everyone fights for at our table.)

Serves 12 to 15 people.

Rochelle Majer Krich's books include *Angel of Death* and *Blood Money*, both featuring LAPD detective Jessica Drake.

Holmes and Hearth

As befitting his British origins, Sherlock Holmes is generally not singled out for his gourmet tastes. Food, in fact, plays little if any role in Conan Doyle's masterworks. But a connection between Holmes and food can be found in at least two far-flung places—some 6,000 miles apart. The proprietors of London's Sherlock Holmes Public House & Restaurant and the Sherlock Holmes Pub-Restaurant in Carmel, California, were both kind enough to send along recipes for some traditional English fare from their menus.

London's Sherlock Holmes Public House & Restaurant is on the site of the Northumberland Hotel, where, Holmes enthusiasts will remember, Sir Henry Baskerville stayed on his visits to London. It is also where Holmes tracked down Francis Hay Moulton in "The Noble Bachelor," and the Turkish baths that Holmes and Watson frequented were right beside the hotel. Visitors to the Sherlock Holmes, which is located at 10-11 Northumberland Street in Westminster (reservations while in London: 0171 930 2644), can see a replica of Holmes' sitting room and study and enjoy Victorian English fare, including Mrs. Hudson's Steak, Ale and Mushroom Pie.

Mrs. Hudson's Steak, Ale and Mushroom Pie

6 tablespoons butter
¾ cup all-purpose flour
1 tablespoon vegetable oil
1 ½ pounds lean diced beef (stewing or braising)
¼ pound mushrooms, sliced
2 large onions, chopped
1 tablespoon tomato paste
16 ounces English ale (dark, if possible)
Packet of ready-made puff/flaky pastry
Salt and pepper to taste

Slowly melt the butter in a saucepan, adding the flour slowly until the roux has a sandy texture. Place to the side, keeping warm.

In a deep saucepan, heat the oil until smoking. Add the diced beef, ensuring the meat is completely sealed, which will retain the meat juices and give the sauce its rich, dark color. Add the mushrooms, onions, and tomato paste, and continue to cook until the onions turn golden. Reduce heat, slowly stir in the ale, ensuring it does not boil over. Simmer for 1 hour to infuse the ale through the meat and to ensure the beef is tender. While the sauce is simmering, roll out the pastry and cut to fit 4 individual pie dishes. Leave to the side.

When the sauce is cooked through, place on low heat and recover the roux. Mix into the sauce slowly until rich and thick, ensuring the sauce is smooth. Add salt and pepper to taste. Divide into pie dishes to just below the surface. Place the precut pastry lids on the pie dishes, brush the lids with egg and/or milk, and cook in the oven at 350 degrees until the pastry lids rise and are golden brown. Serve with roast potatoes and fresh steamed vegetables, or for a lighter meal, fresh steamed vegetables and a spring salad.

Chef's note: If the roux lightens the color of the sauce, darken with 1 to 2 drops of gravy browning (such as Gravy Master).

Serves 4.

> *At each blow the knife, flattened and squared at this point, jumps against the hand and the cook acquires a heavy callus at the base of his forefinger which would have puzzled Sherlock Holmes, who knew no cooks.*
> —Nicolas Freeling, *The Kitchen Book*

While there is no historical record of Sherlock Holmes ever having visited California's Monterey Peninsula, he surely would have loved this little piece of paradise as much as the rest of us. Sherlock Holmes Pub-Restaurant, located at 3772 The Barnyard in Carmel (reservations: 831-625-0340), pays tribute to the sleuth with its wide array of foods from England, many of them cleverly named—the Diogenes Club Sandwich, the Hound of the Baskervilles (a hot dog) and the Bad Actor (ham, of course). Here's their recipe for Victoria Regina Chicken Pie, a favorite.

Victoria Regina Chicken Pie

1 tablespoon olive oil
2 medium onions, chopped
1 ½ pounds fresh mushrooms, sliced
1 tablespoon sweet basil
1 tablespoon oregano
1 tablespoon thyme
10 ounces champagne
4 pounds chicken breast (cut in ¼-inch squares)
5 medium potatoes (cut in ¼-inch squares)
4 carrots, chopped
5 stalks celery, chopped
2 cups water
2 tablespoons chicken base
1 ½ quarts heavy cream
6 tablespoons cornstarch
15 square puff pastry

Heat the oil in a large pot, add the onions, mushrooms, sweet basil, oregano, and thyme. Sauté until the onions are cooked. Add the champagne, let it boil for 2 minutes. Add the chicken, potatoes, carrots, celery, and water. Cook until the chicken and vegetables are done. Add the chicken base, wait 2 minutes, then add the cream. Mix the cornstarch with enough water to dissolve. Add to the boiling mixture for the desired thickness. Serve in individual ovenproof bowls, top with puff pastry, and bake in a 475-degrees oven until puffy and brown.

Serves 15.

NO PLACE TO MEAT

Myron's Potato Latkes

(Gentile translation: Myron's Potato Pancakes)

HARLAN COBEN

*M*y Yoo Hoo-swigging detective Myron Bolitar is not much of a gourmet. His contribution to the culinary arts is usually limited to making observations like "a burger so rare it screamed ouch." This is probably due to the fact that his mother never cooked. But with a little searching, he found this old recipe in the bottom of a drawer.

> 6 medium to large potatoes
> 1 large onion (Vidalia, in season)
> 5 tablespoons flour
> 2 eggs
> 1 teaspoon salt
> ½ teaspoon ground red pepper (cayenne)
> Ground black pepper to taste
> Vegetable oil (to cover bottom of frying pan ¼ inch)

Grate the potatoes (no need to peel) with a mandolin (preferable) or food processor. Try to make the grating as close to shoestrings as possible for the best texture. Boil the grated potatoes in water for 4 minutes. Strain and squeeze dry. Mix in all the other ingredients (except the vegetable oil).

Form the latkes with your hands. Do this by making approximately 3-inch-diameter pancakes and flattening them between the palms of your hands to squeeze out the extra liquid. Place in a frying pan with hot vegetable oil. When golden brown/crispy, flip them over and repeat with the other side. Remove the potato latkes and pat them between paper towels.

Best if served immediately, but they can be kept warm in oven. Make sure you have plenty of sour cream (even nonfat sour cream works well here) and applesauce to accompany. Myron likes them with Yoo Hoo, but you can choose your favorite chocolate drink.

Yields 20 to 25 potato latkes.

Some of the mysteries in Harlan Coben's Edgar, Shamus, and Anthony Award-winning Myron Bolitar series are *The Final Detail, One False Move* and *Fade Away.*

Quick Vegetarian Cassoulet
KATE CHARLES

*T*he following dish is one that Lucy might well cook for David on a cold winter's night. I have adapted this recipe from one I clipped out of a magazine some years ago, and it has become a real standby. In the first place, it can be made entirely from store-cupboard ingredients and things that are already on hand in the fridge. And it is a firm favorite of my husband, who, like David, is a vegetarian by association rather than by personal choice!

Preparation time: 15 minutes

Cooking time: 40 minutes

> 1 tablespoon olive oil
> 1 small onion, chopped
> 2 celery stalks, sliced
> 1 small carrot, chopped
> 1 clove garlic, minced
> 1 small can whole button mushrooms, drained
> 1 14-ounce can mixed beans in tomato sauce
> 1 7-ounce can chopped tomatoes
> 1 teaspoon dried oregano
> 1 tablespoon chopped fresh parsley (or 1 teaspoon freeze-dried)
> 1 ounce cheddar cheese, grated
> 1 ounce ground almonds
> Salt and pepper to taste

Preheat the oven to 400 degrees. Heat the oil in a small flameproof casserole, then add the onion, celery, carrot, and garlic. Cook for 5 minutes, until soft. Stir in the mushrooms, the beans with their sauce, tomatoes, herbs, salt and pepper. Bring to a boil.

Sprinkle the cheese and almonds over the stew, place in the oven, and bake for 30 minutes until golden.

Serve with a green salad and fresh crusty bread.

Serves 2.

Kate Charles' sleuth, Lucy Kingsley, becomes a vegetarian in *The Snares of Death*.

The Lyme House Shepherd's Pie

(Vegetarian)

ELLEN HART

*I*n my Jane Lawless series, Jane owns a restaurant called The Lyme House, which sits on the shore of Lake Harriet in south Minneapolis. This recipe is from her *The Lyme House Cookbook*. Food plays a big part in my all of books—my other series features Sophie Greenway, a part-time restaurant critic and owner of a four-star hotel in St. Paul (complete with two historic restaurants and one theater bar that has been going strong since the early twenties).

> 1 cup *each:* sliced oyster, button, and shitake mushrooms
> ½ cup *each:* carrots, celery, sweet potatoes, parsnips, potato, and onions,
>   all chopped.
> Several pinches of basil, thyme, rosemary, salt and pepper,
>   and tiny amount of sugar to taste
> Whipping cream

Toss all the ingredients and place in a heavy baking pot. Cover with whipping cream.

Bake uncovered at 350 degrees for 1 hour to reduce the sauce—or to the desired consistency (it can bake longer). Taste and adjust the seasoning.

Cover with hot whipped potatoes (mashed with butter, cream, salt, and white pepper).

Sprinkle with paprika.

A professional chef before becoming a writer, Ellen Hart writes 2 series. Her books include *Stage Fright, Hallowed Murder,* and *This Little Piggy Went to Murder.*

Spanakopita
(Spinach Pie)
JUDY AND TAKIS IAKOVOU

*I*n our first book, Julia cites spanakopita as one of her favorite Greek dishes. It is certainly a favorite in our family and has been since Takis and I first met, twenty-four years ago.

Several months after we started dating I decided to surprise him by inviting a few of his friends for a surprise birthday dinner. I was young and naive, not an experienced cook, and no one had ever told me not to serve ethnic food to native Greeks. Not only was I not familiar with the cuisine, I didn't even try a test case! I just jumped into the recipe with no earthly idea how to handle phyllo pastry. The result, which I displayed proudly to both Takis and the guests, was unrecognizable as spanakopita. However, my guests were kind enough to compliment me before explaining how the dish should have been made.

The following recipe is an easier version of same. I find that in working with phyllo it is best to keep it covered with wax paper while buttering the other sheets. I use kitchen scissors to cut the sheets into strips for folding.

> 1 pound frozen phyllo pastry
> 2 10-ounce packages frozen spinach
> 1 pound feta cheese
> 6 eggs, well beaten
> Chopped garlic to taste
> Ground pepper to taste
> 1/4 teaspoon salt
> 1 bunch scallions, chopped
> 1 bunch fresh parsley, chopped
> 1 bunch fresh dill, chopped
> 1/2 to 1 pound butter, melted

Thaw the phyllo for 2 hours, but do not remove from box or inner bag.

Thaw the frozen spinach. You may substitute 1 pound of fresh spinach, steaming 5 minutes or until wilted. Crumble the feta cheese and add the beaten eggs. Add the garlic and ground pepper at will. Mix with the spinach, salt, scallions, and herbs, and set aside.

Unwrap the phyllo, and smooth the sheets flat. Using a sharp knife or scissors, cut vertically in 2-inch strips. Select a 2-to-3 layer thick strip, lay it out vertically, and brush with melted butter. Place a spoonful of filling on the closest end and fold pastry triangularly over the filling. Continue flag-folding to the end. Place on a buttered cookie sheet and begin the next pastry. When all the phyllo/filling is used, butter the top of each pastry individually. Bake 45 minutes at 350 degrees, or until flaky and golden brown. Serve hot.

Restaurateurs Judy Takis Iakovou write the Nick and Julia Lambros mysteries, which include *So Dear To Wicked Men* and *Go Close Against The Enemy*.

Jenny Law's Cheese Soufflé

JANICE LAW

Although Anna got away from an abusive first husband with a well-timed swing of a cast-iron skillet, she has never shown much inclination for cooking, prudently leaving meals to professionals and to her artist husband, Harry.

If she does ever show an interest in the culinary arts, I'll certainly give her this easy and reliable cheese soufflé recipe. Note that the cooking time given produces a moist but not runny soufflé, runny soufflés being, in my Scottish mother's estimation, an undesirable French affectation.

½ cup milk
2 tablespoons Crisco or
    other solid shortening
¼ cup flour
½ pound (2 cups) grated cheese
    (I like extra sharp myself)

4 eggs, separated
Cream of tartar
Salt, pepper, dry mustard

Heat the milk. In a separate saucepan, melt the shortening over moderate heat. Stir in the flour with a wooden spoon to make a smooth paste and to cook the flour. When the milk comes up to the boil, pour it in, stirring with a wire whisk to make a smooth white sauce. It will be thick. Then stir in the grated cheese. Unless you have a really thick saucepan, turn down the heat to low so the cheese won't burn, and stir occasionally. While the cheese melts, beat the egg whites stiffly. A pinch of cream of tartar will help stabilize them.

When the cheese is nicely melted, take the sauce off the heat and add the egg yolks, one at a time, beating with your wooden spoon after each addition. Once the yolks are in, add a good pinch of salt and pepper and, if you like, a pinch of dry mustard.

Stir in a quarter of the egg whites to lighten the batter, then delicately fold in the rest with a spatula. Place the mixture in a well-greased, straight-sided soufflé dish. (I use one that is 7 inches in diameter, which is 6 cups in size.)

Bake at 375 degrees for half an hour.

Serves 2 (can be doubled for 4 servings).

Janice Law is the author of the Anna Peters series which includes *Cross-Check* and *Time Lapse*.

I must go and see Mrs. Medway. Funny how servants cannot
bear the police. Her cheese soufflé last night was quite uneatable.
Soufflés and pastry always show if one is off balance.
    —Agatha Christie, *Murder After Hours*

Eggs à la Chatelaine

D.J. DONALDSON

*I*n *Louisiana Fever* when Andy Broussard, the New Orleans Medical Examiner, goes to the kitchen to prepare his breakfast, Eggs à la Chatelaine is what he's after. Broussard always uses quail eggs in this recipe. Those with a less fastidious palate will find that chicken eggs work just as well. As it happened, Broussard's craving for this treat was thwarted by a call from Homicide, which absorbed so much of this morning he had to settle for eggs Outsellette at Grandma O's, his favorite restaurant. Though he tries repeatedly to sneak a peek while Grandma O makes this latter dish so he might steal her recipe, she has caught him every time. While he eats, he is unaware that a few hours earlier, he inadvertently carried something away from a dead man's apartment that will profoundly change his life.

Bake some tartlets and garnish them with a chestnut puree, to which a puree of Soubise weighing a quarter of the chestnut puree has been added. Arrange soft-boiled or poached eggs on the puree mixture and cover with poultry velouté sauce.

Chestnut puree: Remove the shell of the chestnuts, leaving the inner skin intact. Plunge them in boiling water. Drain and skin. Cook the chestnuts in white stock seasoned with a little celery. (If a meatless puree is required, cook in water.) Drain and rub through a fine sieve. Put the puree in a saucepan and warm, stirring constantly. Just before serving, add fresh butter and a few tablespoons of fresh cream.

Puree Soubise: Blanch 1 pound of sliced onions, drain them, and put in the oven to cook (without a lid) with 3 tablespoons of butter, a pinch of salt, a pinch of white pepper, and a pinch of fine sugar. When the onions are done (without getting colored), add 2 cups of thick béchamel sauce, blend, and cook in the oven with a lid on for 30 minutes. Rub through a sieve, and finish off the puree with 3 tablespoons of butter, whitening it if necessary with several tablespoons of cream.

Béchamel sauce: For 2 ½ quarts, stir 2 ¾ quarts of boiling milk into 1 cup of white roux made of butter and flour. Mix well. Add 5 ounces of diced lean veal, and cook in butter without coloring with 4 tablespoons of chopped onion. Season, add a sprig of thyme, a fragment of bay leaf, and a little grated nutmeg. Simmer very gently for 45 minutes to 1 hour. Strain through a cloth.

White roux: Cook equal parts of flour and clarified butter for 5 minutes, stirring occasionally with a wooden spoon.

Velouté sauce: For 2 ½ quarts, stir 2 ¾ quarts of white stock made with chicken into 1 cup of white roux made with butter and flour. Blend well. Bring to a boil, stirring with a wooden spoon until the first bubbles appear. Cook the sauce very slowly for 1 ½ hours, skimming frequently. Strain through a cloth. Stir until it is completely cold.

D.J. Donaldson's Andy Broussard and Kit Franklin mysteries include *Sleeping with Crawfish, Louisiana Fever,* and *Blood on the Bayou.*

Notorious Nut Burgers
NICOLA FURLONG

After an arduous day pondering peculiar plots, curious clues, and charismatic characters, my little grey cells need recharging. I may be famished, but my culinary interest boarded the "4:50 to Paddington" ages ago. That's when I thank the Great Detective in the Sky for this simple, tasty recipe. One bite of a Notorious Nut Burger and mysterious ideas begin to germinate.

    1 egg
    1 cup finely chopped almonds
    ¼ cup cottage cheese
    ½ cup whole wheat bread crumbs
    1 clove garlic, minced (optional, I prefer to ward off vampires with
        my trusty wooden cross)
    2 tablespoons sesame seeds
    1 tablespoon chopped fresh parsley
    1 tablespoon chopped onion
    1 teaspoon soy sauce
    ¼ teaspoon thyme leaves
    ¼ cup milk
    1 tablespoon sunflower or cooking oil

In a medium-size bowl, combine ingredients except the oil and mix well.

Form mixture into 4 patties, each ½-inch thick. In a large skillet, heat the oil. Cook the patties over medium heat, about 2 minutes on each side, until lightly browned. Stuff your buns with deadly accouterments such as killer ketchup, murderous mustard, and hellishly hot peppers.

4 zesty servings to die for!

Nicola Furlong is the author of *A Hemorrhaging of Souls* and *Teed Off!*, both set on Vancouver Island, British Columbia.

FAITHFUL SIDEKICKS

Carrot Halwa

H.R.F. KEATING

Inspector Ghote's wife, Protima, *"...put a hand on his arm. He smelt suddenly a faint whiff of raw onion from the meal she had been preparing. Cooking for him, as she had done ever since the first day of their marriage when, with such pride, she had made what his mother had told her was his favourite dish, sweet carrot halwa. He felt, a sweeping flood-tide, in that single gesture of hers all that the years of their marriage had brought to them in closeness, in affection, in physical togetherness, in love."*

—*Under A Monsoon Cloud*

I, too, surprise, surprise, love in particular sweet things made with what I was brought up to believe were vegetables. A touch of the topsy-turvy, or, as we say in India, the *ulta pulta.* And I like stirring, too, the feeling that you are really cooking. So the longish time you have to stir to make carrot halwa is, for me, a bonus of pleasure.

    1 pound carrots
    1 ¼ pints milk
    8 cardamom seeds
    5 tablespoons oil
    5 tablespoons sugar or honey
    2 tablespoons raisins
    1 tablespoon almonds, blanched, or pistachios, shelled

Put the carrots through the food processor, or laboriously grate them by hand. Put them with the milk and the cardamoms into a pan, as thick on the bottom as you've got and as wide at the top. Cook over a medium heat (reduced if need be), stirring not absolutely continuously but a lot, till no liquid is left. This could take half an hour. Fry the mixture in a frying pan coated in oil—non-stick is best—stirring away again till the carrots go from looking milky to a rich translucent red, probably as long as a quarter of an hour. Then add the sugar or honey and the raisins and nuts and stir for a couple of minutes more. Serve. Or let it get cold, put it in the fridge and have it, chilled, whenever.

H.R.F. Keating, holder of the Crime Writers Association Cartier Diamond Dagger, is the creator of Inspector Ghote of the Bombay Police, who appears in *Asking Questions*, among other mysteries.

Making-It-Up-As-You-Go Potato Salad

MAXINE O'CALLAGHAN

*O*nce upon a time, back before I became a full-time writer, I made everything from scratch, following recipes and measuring ingredients. These days I find I cook the way I write: I know where I'm going to start and where I'll probably end, and I have a plan for the middle, but freely change things as I go along. My potato salad is a perfect illustration.

Potatoes	Sweet pickle relish
Eggs (hard-boiled, of course!)	Mustard
Onion	Salt and pepper
Mayonnaise	

Allow about 1 potato per serving, more for big eaters or leftovers. Use any kind of potato you like. If you like red potatoes and want to leave the skins on, scrub well. I prefer baking potatoes, the medium-size kind you buy in 5- or 10-pound bags. Pick ones about the same size, and wash the dirt off. Put in a big pot and cover with water.

I figure about 1 egg for every 4 potatoes. You can cook the eggs separately, but why waste water? I put them in with the potatoes. Bring to a boil. Turn down to just above a simmer and cover. After 15 minutes remove the eggs and put in some cool water while the potatoes finish cooking. Time varies with size and variety, but cook until easily pierced by a fork.

Drain the potatoes in a colander until you can handle, then peel. Just use a paper towel if you have to and don't burn your fingers. (I used to cook ahead and refrigerate, but, okay, I confess. A frantic last-minute potato-salad session taught me hot was better.) Chop up the cooked potatoes. Big chunks and slabs, none of that neat cube stuff, and hope the potatoes mush up a little. Trust me, this is good. And put it in a big bowl with room for mixing, but hold off on the mixing until all the ingredients are all in there. Shell the eggs, then hold under running water to get rid of any gritty little pieces. Dry and cut up into the bowl with the potatoes. Add some chopped-up mild onion, a little or a lot to suit your taste.

For you compulsive types, you can mix the dressing in a separate bowl. Being lazy, I just put everything on top of the potato-egg-onion mound. Start with a spoonful of mayo teaspoon, tablespoon, or serving spoon, depending on how many potatoes and how gloppy you like it. The mayo can be light, cholesterol-free, or totally fat-laden. Add some relish, just a dab of mustard my secret ingredient that makes people wonder what I did to make such great stuff. I prefer plain old French's yellow. Experiment if you must. Sprinkle on some salt and pepper.

Mix everything together until the spuds are coated. See how those hot, crumbly potato pieces contribute to a creamy dressing? Not gloppy enough? Repeat with mayo, relish, and mustard until it tastes yummy.

That mayo mixed with the hot potatoes is as good as a culture in a petrie dish for growing nasty things like salmonella, so refrigerate immediately. And enjoy.

Maxine O'Callaghan's series featuring Orange County investigator Delilah West includes *Down for the Count*, *Set-Up*, and *Hit and Run*.

Nellie V.'s Hush Puppies

JAMES D. BREWER

$\mathcal{M}$y Masey Baldridge/Luke Williamson mystery series is set during the 1870s (Reconstruction era) and takes place during the golden age of steamboats along the Mississippi and Ohio rivers. This recipes comes from my dear mother, Mrs. Nellie V. Brewer, and represents old southern family dishes handed down from generation to generation.

This recipe for hush puppies makes a delightful side item to accompany those large, tasty, Mississippi River channel catfish that passengers on the steamboat *Paragon* (featured in all my stories) would have feasted upon in the lavishly furnished grand dining room. Offered to your readers by a third-generation river family, I guarantee you that you'll find no better.

> 1 ½ cups of self-rising cornmeal
> 1 medium onion, chopped fine
> ½ bell pepper, chopped fine
> 1 small can of niblet corn, drained
> 1 cup of buttermilk
> Oil

Mix all the ingredients. Keep the mixture stiff enough to drop by teaspoon into hot fat until golden brown—drain on paper toweling.

James D. Brewer's *No Escape*, *No Bottom*, and *No Justice* all feature Masey Baldridge and Luke Williamson.

Best Fried Green Tomatoes

CHARLAINE HARRIS

*O*f my two Southern series protagonists, Lily Bard and Aurora Teagarden, only one would ever dream of preparing something as depraved (cholesterol-wise) as fried green tomatoes. That one would be Georgia librarian Aurora Teagarden, who has to have them at least once a summer; though her Yankee husband, Martin Bartell, eats only one slice as a courtesy. Aurora doesn't care; that leaves more for her!

> 1 cup all-purpose flour
> 1 cup yellow cornmeal
> 1 teaspoon salt
> ½ teaspoon black pepper
> 2 tablespoons sugar
> 3 medium green tomatoes, unpeeled
> 1 cup buttermilk
> Cooking oil

Mix the flour, cornmeal, salt, pepper, and sugar in a shallow pan. Slice the tomatoes (more thinly for crispier servings). Place a few at a time in the buttermilk. At the same time, be heating the oil in a heavy skillet (iron is best). Roll the soaked slices in the mixture of dry ingredients and fry, one layer at a time, until brown on both sides.

Drain on paper towels.

This recipe makes a gracious plenty.

Charlaine Harris has written five books in the Aurora Teagarden series, including *A Fool and His Honey* and *Dead Over Heels*, and three books in the Lily Bard series, *Shakespeare's Landlord*, *Shakespeare's Champion*, and *Shakespeare's Christmas*.

My Grandmother's Kugel

JODY JAFFE

*T*his recipe for my grandmother's kugel appears in *Chestnut Mare, Beware*. I've been eating it for forty-four years and, despite its ten eggs, pound of cottage cheese, and half pint of sour cream, I'm still alive and writing.

    2 apples
    1 to 2 oranges
    1 lemon
    10 eggs
    1 pound cottage cheese
    2 tablespoons butter
    1 cup sour cream
    1 cup sugar
    1 teaspoon vanilla
    2 pinches nutmeg
    1 cup yellow raisins
    1 pound cooked wide noodles
    Cinnamon sugar

Grate the apples, oranges, and lemon (rinds and all) in a food processor or, if you're a masochist, by hand. In a blender or aforementioned food processor (now empty), mix together everything else except the raisins, noodles, and cinnamon sugar. In a big bowl, combine the grated fruit with the cottage-cheese goop. Mix in the raisins, toss with the cooked noodles, and throw the whole mess in a pan big enough to hold it all—a long lasagna pan works well. Sprinkle with cinnamon sugar and bake at 350 degrees until golden brown—about 1 hour.

Jody Jaffe's mysteries combine her two loves—horses and writing. In addition to *Horse of a Different Killer*, which was nominated for both an Agatha and a Macavity she has also written *Chestnut Mare, Beware* and *In Colt Blood*.

Crumb Potatoes

CAROL CAIL

$\mathcal{M}$y maternal grandmother was not the best of cooks. She tended to boil everything to just this side of combustion. But she did hand me down some unique and yummy recipes, such as this easy one.

Peel enough small potatoes to feed however many will be at dinner. Coat each potato in melted butter or margarine and roll it in fine crackers. Bake on a cookie sheet or pie plate in a 350-degree oven for half an hour. Carefully turn each potato over and bake another half an hour or until it's soft when pricked with a fork.

Carol Cail's series character, Maxey Burnell, has appeared in three novels including *If Two of Them are Dead* and *Unsafe Keeping*.

[Wolfe] explained why it was that all you needed to know about any human society was what they ate. If you know what they ate you could deduce everything else—culture, philosophy, morals, politics, everything....I wondered how you would make out if you tried to deduce everything about Wolfe by knowing what he had eaten in the past ten years. I decided you would deduce that he was dead.

—Rex Stout, *The Final Deduction*

REVENGE IS SWEET

Angelina's Heavenly Layer Cookies

JOANNE PENCE

$\mathcal{M}$y culinary mystery series features gourmet cook Angelina Amalfi. I make no bones about it: I'm not a good cook. In fact, my cooking is fairly awful. However, I come from a family of great cooks, which is what led to my problem. My cooking, you see, has been the family joke for years. I decided to go along with the gag and wrote a book with lots of atrocious recipes in it (my kind of cooking, yes!). The book was *Something's Cooking*. I had expected it to be a single title. Fortunately, though, readers enjoyed the escapades of Angie, and in one of those ironic quirks that happen in real life, I now write a series about a gourmet cook and am learning more about cooking than I ever dreamed. I'm still no Julia Child, but I've become a whiz at reading cookbooks and eating gourmet meals in restaurants.

In my limited "repertoire" of cooking, here's one of my favorite recipes. It's simplicity itself, a deluxe version of the delicious classic seven-layer cookie bar.

    1 stick unsalted butter, melted
    1 ⅓ cups shortbread cookie crumbs (Lorna Doone-type)
    1 ¼ cups walnuts, chopped
    1 ¼ cups shredded coconut
    8 ounces semisweet chocolate bar, cut into chunky shards
    14-ounce can sweetened condensed milk

Pour the melted butter into a 13-by-9-inch pan. Press the cookie crumbs evenly into the butter (this will form the crust for the cookie bars). Scatter the walnuts over the crumbs. Sprinkle ¾ cup of coconut over the nuts. Add the chocolate shards over the coconut. Sprinkle the remaining ½ cup of coconut over the chocolate. Pour the milk over the top and bake at 350 degrees for 20 to 25 minutes, until the milk bubbles and the coconut is golden. Cool and cut into bars.

The Angie Amalfi series includes *Cooks Overboard, Cook's Night Out* and *Cooking Most Deadly*.

Smiling Faces

S.J. ROZAN

*T*his recipe for a Cantonese sweet treat is mentioned in my new book, *A Bitter Feast,* featuring Lydia Chin who recalls:

> *Their warm, rich scent suddenly brought back to me our cramped kitchen and my father's voice. "See how they smile when you cook them?" he'd say, as the balls split in the hot oil. And my mother would reply, "It's a lucky thing the dough is smiling, because all the children in this house are quarrelsome." And my father's face would grow sad. "Quarrelsome, ah? Such a shame. Quarrelsome children cannot eat Smiling Faces."*

1 ½ cups sugar	3 tablespoons lard, softened
¾ cup boiling water	2 eggs
4 cups flour	½ cup sesame seeds
3 teaspoons baking powder	6 cups oil
½ teaspoon baking soda	

Dissolve the sugar in boiling water. Let it cool.

Sift the flour, baking powder, and baking soda onto a kneading board. Make a well in the center, put in the lard and eggs. Pour in the sugar mixture in a gradual stream. Blend well into the dough.

Lightly knead for 30 seconds. Do not overknead. Cover the dough with a kitchen towel and set at room temperature for 20 minutes.

Divide the dough into 4 equal parts. Roll each part by hand to form a long tube, 1 inch in diameter. Break each tube into 10 equal parts.

Take each piece of dough and roll it into a ball. Spread the sesame seeds in a dish and roll each ball in the seeds. Press and roll until the ball's entire surface is covered. Press the seeds in as firmly as possible.

Heat the oil in a wok over medium heat until the oil reaches 300 degrees. (Note: If you don't have a thermometer, test the oil the Chinese way: Drop in a small piece of scallion green. If the oil sizzles and bubbles appear around the green immediately, the oil is ready.)

Add 10 balls; do not stir. Balls will roll and turn in the hot oil and split into Smiling Faces. Deep-fry until golden brown. Remove and drain on paper towels. Repeat with other batches of 10.

Makes 40 Smiling Faces.

In addition to *A Bitter Feast,* S.J. Rozan's books include *No Colder Place, Mandarin Plaid,* and *China Trade.*

Boiled Cookies

L.L. THRASHER

When I was a child, my family lived for a few months in a rented house that came with a broken stove. The burners were fine, but the oven didn't work at all. My mother had always prepared homemade desserts, which were not only better-tasting but were far less expensive than "store-bought" goodies for a family of eight. Without an oven, she was unable to prepare many desserts, including cookies of any type. Her sister, my aunt Alice, gave her the recipe for Boiled Cookies and we enjoyed them frequently. They continue to be a family favorite to this day, even though we all have working ovens now.

 2 cups sugar
 3 tablespoons baking cocoa
 ½ cup milk
 1 tablespoon butter or margarine
 ½ cup peanut butter
 ½ cup chopped walnuts
 3 cups uncooked oatmeal
 1 teaspoon vanilla

Have ready a lightly buttered 9-by-13-inch pan.

Combine the sugar, cocoa, milk, and butter or margarine in a large saucepan. Bring the sugar/cocoa mixture to a boil. Boil for 1 minute. Quickly stir the peanut butter, nuts, oatmeal, and vanilla into the chocolate mixture. Quickly spread into the 9-by-13-inch pan. Cut into squares when cool. (If you prefer, the cookie dough can be dropped by rounded spoonfuls onto a lightly buttered cookie sheet; work rapidly because the mixture sets quickly.)

L. L. Thrasher is the author of the Zachariah Smith mysteries *Cat's-Paw, Incorporated* and *Dogsbody, Incorporated* and the Lizbet Lange mystery, *Charlie's Bones.*

Rita Rak's Butter Cookies
BARBARA D'AMATO

*M*y detective, Cat Marsala is hired by Bruno Angelotti, owner of the finest (fictional) food market in Chicago, Spenser and Angelotti, to investigate the discovery of a human bone in the meat case. Working in the catering end of the business Cat listens to what people are saying…and gets to enjoy some of the treats made by the baker for Spenser and Angelotti's staff break room, including these cookies.

> 1 pound butter
> 1 cup sugar
> 2 egg yolks
> 1 teaspoon vanilla
> 4 cups flour

Cream the butter and sugar. Add the egg yolks and vanilla. Gradually add the flour. Place rounded shapes on an ungreased cookie sheet and flatten with a fork. Bake at 350 degrees for about 10 to 12 minutes.

Deceptively simple, this cookie is simply delicious. It can be varied by adding grated lemon peel or orange peel, but you really don't need to gild this lily. Because it is a stiff dough, it can be formed into wreaths or other shapes for holidays or put through a cookie press.

Among Barbara D'Amato's mysteries are *Hard Evidence*, *Hardball* and *KILLER.app*.

Tea with Dame Agatha

Nibbling delicately at a scone and balancing a cup of tea on his knee, Hercule Poirot allowed himself to become confidential with his hostess.

—from *The Labors of Hercules*

*W*ithout argument, two diversions the British have down to an art are the seamless whodunit and the fine tradition of afternoon tea. For those of us weaned on Conan Doyle, Sayers, Chesterton, and Allingham, reading a good mystery and savoring a cup of tea can seem almost inseparable pleasures.

Though her father was in fact American, Agatha Christie has come to embody the quintessential purveyor of murder most English in most everyone's mind. And it would be hard to read any one of her more than eighty books without encountering someone who avails himself of a teatime respite.

Whenever she was in London for the day, Agatha Christie would take her tea at the venerable Brown's Hotel in Mayfair. There, in the enviably placid age before cellular phones, she would *do her telephoning* while enjoying (we presume) a pot of tea and some of the hotel's tasty offerings. And we like to believe that Dame Agatha hatched more than one of her diabolically clever plots while munching on tea cakes and scones at Brown's.

Gregory Nicholson, chef de cuisine at 1837, the new restaurant at Brown's, was kind enough to contribute the recipe for the afternoon-tea scone that are baked and served today at the hotel in the definitive English tradition. We've adapted the recipe for this simple but delectable basic for the home cook. Next time you're in London, though, stop in and enjoy the real thing at 1837, Brown's Hotel, Albemarle Street, Mayfair (reservations: 0171 408 1837).

Brown's Hotel Afternoon-Tea Scones

3 ½ cups all-purpose flour
2 tablespoons baking powder
¼ pound butter
6 tablespoons sugar
2 eggs
¼ cup milk
¼ cup sultanas (or golden raisins)

Preheat the oven to 375 degrees. In a large bowl, sift the flour and baking powder twice. Add the butter, and crumb the mixture. Whisk together the sugar, eggs, and milk, and add to the flour mixture. Combine the ingredients until they make a firm dough. Carefully add the sultanas. Allow the dough to rest for 15 to 20 minutes.

Roll out the dough on a floured board, ¼-to-½-inch thickness, and cut into 3-inch rounds with a biscuit cutter. Place on a lightly greased cookie sheet. Bake 10 to 12 minutes.

Yields 12 scones.

To Brew a Perfect Pot of English Tea

Start with *fresh* water from the cold tap, not water that's been sitting on the stove, left over from the last time. Just before the kettle boils, pour about a cup's worth of the hot water into your teapot and swirl it around to warm the inside of the pot, then pour that water away. Why? Because warming the pot will keep the boiling water you're about to add from cooling too quickly, and the tea leaves will then steep properly.

Into the warmed pot, measure 1 teaspoon of good-quality black tea leaves for each person and 1 teaspoon "for the pot." Fill the pot with boiling water (be careful not to overboil the water, which depletes the oxygen and will make the tea bitter). The tea should be allowed to brew for 3 to 5 minutes, depending on the size of the leaves (the larger the leaf, the longer the steeping). Stir the tea and pour it into cups, using a strainer.

If you like milk in your tea—as nearly everyone in the British Isles does—add it to the cup *before* the tea.

> *Will you have a hot scone or a sandwich, or this cake? We have*
> *an Italian cook and she makes quite good pastry and cakes. You see,*
> *we have taken to your English afternoon tea....*
> —from *The Mirror Crack'd*

Lavender and Old Malice Cookies

SUSAN WITTIG ALBERT

$\mathcal{T}$his recipe comes from the eighth China Bayles herbal mystery, *Lavender and Old Malice*. Lavender has always been one of my favorite herbs—I grow it, drink it, sleep on it, take baths in it, stow it in the linen closet. After a long day at the computer, a handful of lavender cookies and a cup of lavender tea don't just taste good, they're actually soothing. (For 2,000 years, lavender has been used to calm fits of madness—and I usually feel a little crazy after a day's work.) But traditionally, snakes love the plant and curl around it, waiting to strike. So be careful—lavender smells sweet and tastes good, but malice may be lurking at the root!

½ cup shortening
1 cup sugar
2 eggs
½ teaspoon vanilla
1 tablespoon finely chopped, organically grown lavender flowers
1 ½ cups flour
½ cup finely chopped almonds
2 teaspoons baking powder

Preheat the oven to 350 degrees. Cream the shortening and sugar in a large bowl. Beat in the eggs and vanilla. Stir in the dry ingredients and nuts until well-blended. Drop by teaspoons on a greased cookie sheet and bake for 8 to 10 minutes.

Among the mystery novels by Susan Wittig Albert are *Lavender and Old Malice* and *Love Lies Bleeding*.

Hazelnut Snickerdoodles

PAULA GOSLING

$\mathscr{A}$lthough I am English-domiciled, I returned to my Michigan roots a few years ago with my mystery series set in the Great Lakes resort town of Blackwater Bay. There, a tree-enshrouded spit of land called Paradise Island shelters ten substantial summer cottages that have been treasured by the same families for almost a century. I hope fans of my atmospheric whodunits can easily imagine lounging on one of the lakeside porches on a quiet afternoon, savoring a few of these cookies along with a cup of coffee or a glass of ice-cold milk—and a good mystery, of course. A perfect day, which could be spoiled only by a uninvited corpse.

Set the oven to 400 degrees.

Mix thoroughly:

> 1 cup soft shortening (at least ½ butter)
> 1 ½ cups granulated sugar
> 2 eggs

Sift together and stir in:

> 2 ¾ cups sifted flour
> 2 teaspoons cream of tartar
> 1 teaspoon baking soda
> ¼ teaspoon salt

Add:

> ¾ cup chopped toasted hazelnuts

In a separate bowl blend and set aside:

> 3 tablespoons cinnamon
> 3 tablespoons sugar

Roll the dough into balls, using about 1 tablespoon of dough at a time—making balls about the size of a cherry tomato. Roll the balls in the cinnamon and sugar mixture until completely covered. Place 2 inches apart on an ungreased baking sheet. Bake for 8 to 10 minutes, until very lightly browned but still soft. (They will puff up at first, then flatten out.) Give them a moment to cool before removing them to an area you have covered first with newspaper and then with paper towels. Allow to cool completely.

Should make about 60 cookies.

A past chairman of the British Crime Writers' Association, Paula Gosling has published 12 mystery novels, among them her Blackwater Bay series, which includes *The Body in Blackwater*, *A Few Dying Words* and *The Dead of Winter*.

Persimmon Cookies

JONNIE JACOBS

This recipe is a tradition in our family and one my sleuth, Kate Austen, would make as well, because it's easy. Persimmon trees are abundant in the San Francisco East Bay area, where I grew up (and where Kate now lives). My parents have a prolific one in their back yard, which may explain why the cookies are a family tradition. Neither Kate nor I is much for baking, but these cookies are simple to make and so good, they're always a hit.

1 cup sugar
½ cup margarine
1 egg
1 cup persimmon pulp (about 3 ripe persimmons)
1 teaspoon baking soda
1 teaspoon cinnamon
1 teaspoon nutmeg
1 teaspoon cloves
Dash of salt
2 cups flour
1 cup raisins
1 cup nuts

Cream the sugar and margarine with an electric mixer or food processor. Add the egg, persimmon pulp, baking soda, cinnamon, nutmeg, cloves, and salt. Blend. Add the flour, then the raisins and nuts.

Drop by the teaspoonful onto a cookie sheet. Bake in a 350-degree oven for 15 minutes. (Recipe can be doubled.)

In addition to the Kate Austen series, which includes *Murder Among Us* and *Murder Among Friends,* Jonnie Jacobs also writes the Kali O'Brien series which has included *Motion To Dismiss* and *Evidence of Guilt.*

Aunt Nanette's "S" Cookies

RICHARD BARTH

$\mathcal{M}$argaret Binton, the heroine in seven of my books, loves to bake cookies. She is not unlike the millions of other senior citizens to whom cooking serves as a delightful way to both spend time and create something delicious. But unlike all the rest, to Margaret, cookies are also a weapon, a way to ingratiate herself into the inner sanctum of police power. Lieutenant Morley can't refuse her offerings of delicate molasses-laced cookies and so winds up allowing her into his office, into his cases, and grudgingly, into his heart. And as good as her cookies are, her advice is even better, which is perhaps why the cops in Morley's precinct house tolerate her special brand of New York insouciance and cheek.

Paper-thin molasses cookies are incredibly difficult to pull off. The timing has to be so exquisitely perfect that if the phone rings and one is foolish enough to answer it, an hour of preparation is shot in the time it takes to hurriedly say, "Sorry, I'll have to call you back." So, I'll leave them to Margaret, who seems to have a great way with timing. The following is a family recipe for a different kind of cookie, a hardier varietal which has more latitude in the timing. You might even take in a weather or traffic report and still pull out a perfect batch. The recipe has been delighting first-, second-, and third-generation Barths for years, and I offer it here as a tribute to the woman who brought it with her from Flehingen, Germany, over sixty years ago. I call them Aunt Nanette's "S" cookies.

> 1 egg
> ½ pound butter at room temperature, cut into mixture of:
>> 1 cup sugar
>> 1 ½ cups sifted flour
>> 1 teaspoon vanilla
>> Pinch of salt
>> ½ teaspoon baking powder

Mix everything together to a dough (you can use your hands) and then put in a cookie press. Using a small star-type attachment in the press, make thin strips of cookies on a greased sheet. Cut the strips into approximately 2-inch strips and form into "S" shape. (If there is a 5-year-old or thereabouts in the house, you can also make "O"s, "U"s, "J"s, etc., and proceed to teach the alphabet, although, frankly, the "S"s taste the best.)

Cook in a preheated oven at 350 degrees for 5-plus minutes. (Watch carefully. If you must get a weather report, use the radio, not the television.) This recipe, as my sister attests, make a lot. If you double the recipe, be prepared to spend the afternoon in a hot kitchen and then the rest of the evening trying to get the letter "S" out of your head. But everyone will love them, and who knows, a handful in the right quarters might even fix a parking ticket.

Richard Barth's Margaret Binton appears in *The Condo Kill* and *Deathics*.

Rose Hip Jam

(Tastes of Roses and Is Loaded with Vitamins)

KAREN HARPER

*T*udor roses play a prominent part in my series, The Bess Tudor Mysteries, which features Queen Elizabeth I as the amateur sleuth. Authentic trappings of those times are woven throughout the novels, including food made from roses. Although the first in the series, *The Poyson Garden*, features victims poisoned with food (!), this excellent recipe is entirely safe.

Before becoming a full-time writer, I taught British Literature, and each year my high-school seniors put on an Elizabethan Festival, offering some authentic recipes—both the tasty and the gross. The one which follows is delightful enough to please Her Majesty herself. Even if the Virgin Queen's teeth supposedly turned black because of her love of sugared treats, fear not.

> 1 quart rose hips—best if touched by frost
> 1 quart of water
> 1 pound sugar for each pound of strained rose hip pulp

Wash the hips and remove the calyxes (external green "petal" parts surrounding the hips). Place in a stew pot with water and boil until tender, mashing with a spoon or old-fashioned potato masher. Force the pulp through a colander for better consistency and to remove the seeds. Boil the sugar and pulp together until the jelly thermometer registers 212 degrees. Place in sterilized jars and cover with sealed tops. These make beautiful gifts with a bit of flower-printed cloth tied with ribbon or yarn over the top.

The Poyson Garden is the first in Karen Harper's new Bess Tudor historical mystery series.

> *Myron sipped his coffee. Gourmet coffee. A year ago he never drank coffee. Then he started stopping into one of the new coffee bars that kept cropping up like bad movies on cable. Now Myron could not go through a morning without his gourmet coffee fix.*
> *There is a fine line between a coffee house and a crack house.*
> —Harlan Coben, *One False Move*

Mae Menville's Mardi Gras Cakes
MALCOLM K. SHUMAN

In chapter one of my archaeological mystery *Burial Ground*, Alan Graham and his client, T-Joe, are seated in a café in downtown Baton Rouge eating beignets. Beignets are fried, puffed rolls similar to the *sopapilla* of the American Southwest. They are sprinkled with powdered sugar and served with coffee or hot chocolate. They are a staple at the famous French Market Café in New Orleans. The following, however, is the recipe of my late grandmother, Mae Menville, which exists only as a wrinkled sheet of notebook paper with spidery handwriting. My grandmother called beignets "Mardi Gras Cakes" because she made them once a year, on Mardi Gras day. They can, however, be enjoyed all year-round and you don't have to be a Cajun or a Creole.

> 1 yeast cake
> 2 cups scalded milk
> 2 tablespoons of butter, softened
> ½ cup sugar
> Pinch of salt
> Flour
> 5 eggs, well-beaten
> Lard (or oil)

Dissolve the yeast cake in scalded milk. Add 2 tablespoons of butter, 1 tablespoon of the sugar, a pinch of salt, and enough flour to make a thin, pancake-like batter. Set aside and let rise for about 30 to 40 minutes. Then add the eggs, remaining sugar, and more flour to reach a bread-dough consistency. Work the batter out on a board. Put the batter back in a greased bowl and let rise again. When ready, pull of small plum-size pieces of dough and press out with your fingertips on the bread board—should be lumpy. Cook the pieces in hot lard or oil until light brown and puffed. Drain and sprinkle with powdered sugar.

Makes about a dozen.

Malcolm K. Shuman, like his protagonist Alan Graham in *Burial Ground*, practices contract archaeology. As M.K. Shuman and M.S. Karl his books include *Deep Kill*, *Maya Stone* and *Stone Murders*.

Criminally Delicious Caramel Squares
DENISE OSBORNE

While I attended high school in Japan in the early 1960's, my mother took cooking lessons taught by the Benedictine nuns of Tokyo. Among the fabulous dishes Mother learned to prepare was the dessert that follows, a delicious concoction of caramel meringue, walnuts, and moist cake. When my French class held a cooking contest, I entered this cake and won second prize, actually an unofficial first, since first prize went to a confectionery construction of the Eiffel Tower, much oohed but uneaten.

½ cup shortening
½ cup sugar
3 eggs, separated (all yolks together, 2 whites and 1 white separated)
1 teaspoon vanilla
1 cup flour (sifted together with 1 teaspoon baking powder)
¼ teaspoon salt
3 tablespoons milk
¾ cup chopped walnuts
1 ¾ cups light brown sugar
½ teaspoon vanilla

Preheat the oven to 350 degrees. Cream together the shortening and sugar. Add 3 egg yolks and 1 egg white. Beat well. Add 1 teaspoon vanilla, flour/baking powder, salt, and milk. Spread this mixture in a well-greased and lightly floured 12-by-8-by-2-inch baking dish. Sprinkle with chopped nuts.

Beat 2 egg whites until stiff. Add the brown sugar and ½ teaspoon of vanilla. Spread this mixture over the nuts.

Bake for 30 minutes, then cover with foil and bake an additional 30 minutes. Cut into squares while warm.

Denise Osborne's *Murder Offscreen* and *Cut To: Murder* feature screenwriter-sleuth Queenie Davilov. She is at work on a new series featuring a Nisei fêng shui practitioner.

Special New York Bars
CAROLYN WHEAT

You're walking down Court Street, away from Brooklyn Heights and the courthouses. You cross Atlantic Avenue, home of Middle Eastern restaurants and the Brooklyn House of Detention. Next to the Korean market, you see a brownstone with gold lettering on the parlor floor window: CASSANDRA JAMESON, COUNSELOR AT LAW. The ground floor houses the Morning Glory Natural Foods Luncheonette, where Dorinda Blalock stands behind the counter in her Mom Walton apron, trying to interest her best friend Cass in a glass of herbal tea.

No way. Cass is a confirmed coffee drinker, even in the face of Dorinda's opinion that "coffee is a drink of anger." She drinks it hot, she drinks it iced, and, most of all, she drinks it with chocolate in any form. Since Cass isn't just a friend but the landlord, Dorinda occasionally relaxes her health-food principles to create a rich, sensuous, politically incorrect dessert certain to shoot her friend's cholesterol through the roof. Perfect with coffee, almost-perfect without coffee, Special New York Bars hit the spot with any chocolate lover.

There will be 3 layers.

Layer 1:

Grease an 8-inch square pan and set aside.

Mix the following together in a bowl:

1 ½ cups graham cracker crumbs	¾ cup broken nutmeats
1 cup coconut	(I prefer pecans)

Melt over hot water (remember double boilers?):

½ cup butter (not a politically correct recipe)	3 tablespoons cocoa
¼ cup sugar	

When thoroughly melted and blended, remove from heat and add (slowly) 1 beaten egg and 1 teaspoon of vanilla. Pour the mixture into the dry ingredients and mush it all up. Mash into the square pan as a crust; refrigerate.

Layer 2:

Add 1 ½ cups of sifted powdered sugar to ¼ cup softened butter, then add 2 to 3 tablespoons of cream and blend into a paste. Spread on the refrigerated crust and put back in refrigerator until set.

Layer 3:

Melt 3 squares of unsweetened chocolate and spread over the top; put it back in the refrigerator until hard.

Cut, serve, eat, and go straight to chocolate-lover's heaven. These are messy to eat and take time to make, but you can't eat just one.

Carolyn Wheat is the author of the Cass Jameson legal mysteries, including *Sworn to Defend.* She is also known for her short stories and is the winner of the Agatha, Anthony, Macavity, and Shamus awards for her short fiction.

Parker Dann's Bitchin' Good Brownies
(Niggled from His Friends Nadia and Sylvia)
CHRIS ROGERS

My first suspense novel, *Bitch Factor*, features bounty hunter Dixie Flannigan and Parker Dann, who makes the best brownies Dixie's ever sunk a tooth into. Parker niggled the recipe from his good friends Nadia and Sylvia, and he parts with it only to be part of this special collection.

    4 ounces unsweetened chocolate
    1 cup (2 sticks) unsalted sweet butter
    1 heaping cup flour
    2 cups sugar
    ½ teaspoon baking powder
    ½ teaspoon salt
    4 eggs
    2 teaspoons vanilla
    1 cup pecans, chopped

Preheat the oven to 350 degrees. Grease a 13-by-9-inch cake pan; set aside.

Melt the chocolate and butter together in the top of a double boiler set over hot water. Stir the flour, sugar, baking powder, and salt together. Add the chocolate mixture, then beat the eggs in one at a time. Add the vanilla and the pecans. Pour into a prepared pan and bake for 30 minutes. Cool and spread on the frosting.

Frosting

    ½ cup (1 stick) unsalted sweet butter
    2 squares unsweetened chocolate
    ¼ cup sugar
    2 tablespoons water
    2 ½ cups powdered sugar
    1 egg

Melt the butter and chocolate together in the top of a double boiler set over hot water. In another pan, boil the sugar and water 1 minute. Stir into the butter-chocolate mixture. Let it cool. Beat the powdered sugar and egg, then blend with the cooled chocolate mixture. Beat until smooth and creamy. Spread over the brownies. Allow to set, then cut.

Makes about 36 brownies.

In addition to *Bitch Factor*, Chris Rogers has also written *Rage Factor*, the second in the series featuring Former state prosecutor turned bounty hunter, Dixie Flannigan.

Father John O'Malley's Heavenly Brownies
MARGARET COEL

Father John slipped a brownie onto the edge of his plate between the slice of pork and the potato salad. He never got used to the way Westerners piled food together, but the brownie looked too good to pass up.

—from *The Eagle Catcher*

¼ pound margarine
1 cup sugar
4 eggs
1 teaspoon vanilla
1 1-pound can chocolate syrup
1 cup plus 1 tablespoon flour
½ cup ground nuts (walnuts or pecans)

Cream the margarine and sugar together. Add the eggs, beating after each one. Stir in the rest of the ingredients. Pour into a greased 10-by-15-inch pan. Bake 30 minutes at 350 degrees. Remove from the oven and immediately pour hot frosting over the top.

Frosting

5 tablespoons margarine
6 tablespoons milk
1 ½ cups sugar
½ cup chocolate chips

Boil the first 3 ingredients hard for 30 seconds. Remove from heat and add the chocolate chips. Stir until melted.

Margaret Coel's series about Father John O'Malley and his Arapaho parishioners includes *The Story Teller*, *The Dream Stalker*, and *The Ghost Walker*.

"That's a good, stout-looking pot. Has it got any more in it?"
"Yes, indeed," said Miss Climpson, eagerly. "My dear father used to say I was a great hand at getting the utmost out of a tea-pot. The secret is to fill up as you go and never empty the pot completely."
—Dorothy L. Sayers, *Strong Poison*

Madame Mallais' Old Victorian Ginger Cakes
SARAH SMITH

*M*y first editor, Bob Wyatt, sent me this recipe a couple of weeks before Christmas, by e-mail, with the subject line: *You have to try this NOW! NOW! NOW!* (The e-mail had been sent, as I recall, about 1:00 A.M.) I did try them, and they immediately became a favorite Christmas cookie. I was so taken with them that, as a joke for Bob, I wrote them into *The Knowledge of Water*, where Madame Mallais serves them to Perdita. They are buttery, ginger-flavored, and rather Dickensian.

Madame Mallais doesn't use a food processor, since she was cooking in 1910, but the rest of us do.

> 1 ⅓ cups old-fashioned oats (but instant will do in a pinch)
> 1 cup whole-wheat flour, or ordinary white flour if you prefer
> 1 ⅓ tablespoons dried ground ginger.
>   (Do not use the pale tasteless stuff you've had in the closet since Chester A.
>   Arthur's inaugural. Go out and get it fresh-ground from a natural-foods store.)
> ¼ teaspoon baking powder
> 2 cups dark brown sugar
> 10 tablespoons butter (really 10 tablespoons, not a stick)

Grind all the dry ingredients together in the food processor, then cut the butter up in roughly 1-tablespoon chunks, dump it in, and process until it all is vaguely sticking together. Dump out onto a 12-by-16 ungreased, rimmed cookie sheet. Pat down evenly to ¼- to ⅓-inch thickness.

Bake at 350 degrees for 15 minutes. Cool in the pan for 5 minutes, then cut into 1 ½-inch squares. Allow to cool completely before removing from pan. Pack in tins when cool.

Note: Save crumbs from the first batch, mix in a little white sugar and ginger, and sprinkle onto the next batch after they have baked for 11 minutes.

Sarah Smith is the author of *New York Times* Notable Books and best-sellers *The Vanished Child* and *The Knowledge of Water*.

Martin Altamirano's Hot Chocolate

KEITH SNYDER

*M*artin makes a far less potent version of this in *Coffin's Got the Dead Guy on the Inside*, my most recent Jason Keltner book. There are no measurements. Add pinches and keep tasting it until it's so rich and sweet that you're not sure you can drink a whole mug.

Of course, I'm leaving out a critical ingredient, because this is what compelled La Diva to marry me, and I do not want such awesome power raging undiluted in the world.

> Milk
> A lot of Ibarra or Abuela (Mexican chocolate with cinnamon),
>   broken into pieces
> Vanilla extract (Cook's, if you can find it)
> Stuff from your cabinets
> A pinch of salt
> A dollop of Kahlua
> Whipped cream (the real kind you make, not the plastic by-product
>   that comes in squirt cans)

Heat the milk in a saucepan, but don't let it boil. When it's good and hot, pour about a cup of it into a blender with more Ibarra pieces than are called for by recipe on the package. Blend until blended. Don't use all the Ibarra. Pour the mixture back into the saucepan with the rest of the milk and keep it on medium heat, whisking it constantly. Add just barely enough vanilla.

Go through your cabinets and pull out anything that seems as though it might go with chocolate. Powdered ginger, nutmeg, cloves, allspice, and almond extract are all good. Mint and orange extracts aren't. You probably have other stuff I haven't thought of. Put it all in there. The worst that happens is you make it too strong. If that does happen, add more milk.

Add a pinch of salt just to balance all the sweet stuff. Not too much.

Some Kahlua is probably enough.

When it tastes like cherubim are serenading your tongue, pour it through a strainer into mugs. (Nutmeg is too woody for drinking, eggnog notwithstanding.) Spoon whipped cream onto it, grate the remaining chunk of Ibarra over the whipped cream, and serve to your intended.

Keith Snyder is the author of *Show Control* and *Coffin's Got the Dead Guy on the Inside*.

JUST DESSERTS

Elizabeth MacPherson's Queen Elizabeth Cake
SHARYN MCCRUMB

*E*lizabeth MacPherson is the forensic anthropologist sleuth in eight of my mystery novels. Her recipe for Queen Elizabeth Cake is offered as a letter from MacPherson to her brother:

Dear Bill:

I cannot think why you agreed to take a dessert to the Young Lawyers' Social, unless the others want to get in a little practice suing for damages to their taste buds. I would have expected you to take your usual buffet staple: cartoon napkins and plastic folks. But then, I suppose that your law partner, who could enter the Miss America contest as Ms. Visigoth, probably bagged that contribution, and now you are driven to cook. Poor Bill.

Well, like the good sister I am, I have managed to obtain for you a highly prestigious and coveted cake recipe. According to Cameron's mother, this recipe belongs to Queen Elizabeth herself, though when she finds time to cook I don't know. I hope you are properly impressed. Incidentally, Bill, you cannot do this in a toaster oven. Try to find someone who has a real kitchen.

Here's the recipe. Take 1 cup of boiling water—get someone to explain to you how to do this—and pour it over a cup of chopped dates. (The kind you buy in the grocery store, as opposed to the kind you don't have.) Add a teaspoon of baking soda. Let that mixture stand while you mix the following ingredients (The Queen probably has a scullery maid do this):

> 1 cup of sugar
> ¼ cup butter, softened
> 1 beaten egg
> 1 teaspoon vanilla
> ⅓ teaspoon salt
> ⅓ cup chopped nuts

Add the mixture to the date goo, alternating with 1 ½ cups of flour mixed with 1 teaspoon of baking powder. (There is a difference between baking soda and baking powder. We don't have to get philosophical about this as long as you use the one you're told to.)

Pour the whole thing into an 8-by-10-inch pan and bake in a 375-degree oven for 35 minutes. (A Bundt pan makes a nicely shaped cake, but I know that you think a Bundt is a German political association, so never mind.)

Icing

You can top this cake with powdered sugar if you are too lazy to actually make an icing. The rest of us combine 5 tablespoons of brown sugar, 3 tablespoons of butter, and 3 tablespoons of milk. Boil 3 minutes, cool, beat until the mixture thickens.

If you can talk Mother into letting you use the Spode china and the family silver, the cake will be quite impressive—but since you will be serving this at a gathering of fellow attorneys, be sure to count the forks.

According to Cameron's mother, the Queen requests that you pay a "royalty" each time you use her recipe, by donating one pound sterling to a charity. (That's about $1.55 at the moment.) You ought to send yours to the Legal Aid Society.

Bon Appétit!

Your talented sister,

Elizabeth

Sharyn McCrumb is a *New York Times* best-selling author of three vastly different mystery series, including the Agatha-winning *She Walks These Hills* (one of the Ballad Books). Her other books include *The Ballad of Frankie Silver* and *If I'd Killed Him When I Met Him.*

Parkin

JONATHAN GASH

This traditional recipe originated in Lancashire, England, where I was born and raised. This is a somewhat heavy cake but is simply the best cake ever made since the entire history of the world began (honest!). Traditionally, it is eaten on Bonfire Night, the night we celebrate the execution (sic!) of one Guy Fawkes, who four hundred years ago failed in his attempt to blow up our Houses of Parliament. The day is observed with bonfires and fireworks everywhere. The bonfire tradition actually predates the supposed origin, for its date is said to coincide with that of a primitive ritual of the ancient Britons, but its folklore was given the newer gloss in 1605. Parkin cake was always distributed when the "Guy," a scarecrow-type figure made of stuffed rags, was cast onto the fire at the height of the celebrations. It sounds rather sinister but is always festive. (In the East Anglian village where I live, a huge bonfire, with a fireworks party, is held on the village green, as everywhere else.) However, we have to make our own Lancashire parkin at home!

Strangely, it comes to memory as I write this that I have never seen parkin cut into anything other than small rectangles. I recall my gran rebuking me when I was a little lad for trying to hack a corner off her parkin. She clipped my ear with the admonition, "Triangles isn't for parkin. Parkin comes square!"

(*Nota bene*: Parkin was sometimes also called "tharf cake," but this term meant other types of cake also and is mostly obsolete.)

> 2 ounces soft brown sugar
> 4 ounces lard
> 8 ounces black treacle (or half treacle and honey)
> 8 ounces oatmeal (*not* porridge oats, please)
> 3 ounces plain flour
> 1 level teaspoon ground ginger
> 2 teaspoons bicarbonate of soda dissolved in 3 fluid ounces milk

Melt the sugar, lard, and treacle (or the treacle and honey) over a low heat. Cool it a little. Mix the oatmeal, flour, and ginger in a bowl. Add the cooled treacle mixture. Add the bicarbonate of soda dissolved in milk. Mix well. Pour into a lined, greased roasting tin. Bake for 90 minutes at 300 degrees. Cool before turning out.

Jonathan Gash's mysteries featuring antiques dealer Lovejoy include *The Possessions of a Lady, The Gondola Scam,* and *The Sin Within Her Smile* and have served as the inspiration for the long-running *Lovejoy* television series.

Cynthia's Pecan Praline Cake

J.A. JANCE

Every Christmas a friend who was born and reared in Texas sends me several pounds of Texas pecans. In order to see that none of those precious nuts goes to waste, she also passed along a recipe for Pecan Praline Cake. It quickly became a family-wide favorite.

During the third Joanna Brady book, *Shoot/Don't Shoot*, several of my characters attended a post-church-service coffee hour. One of the things that makes writing fun is the ability to put in what I personally like. Consequently, it was only natural that Jennifer Brady would scarf down several pieces of my favorite cake. Also not surprisingly, the character who brought the fictional cake to the fictional coffee hour just happens to have the same name as the woman who sends me the pecans. Herewith is the recipe for Cynthia's Pecan Praline Cake.

Cake:

1 cup dry oatmeal
1 cup cold water
1 cup sugar
1 ½ cups brown sugar
2 eggs
1 cup oil
1 ½ cups flour
1 teaspoon baking soda
1 teaspoon cinnamon
¼ teaspoon salt

Icing

1 stick butter
3 tablespoons milk
1 ½ cups packed brown sugar
1 ½ cups chopped pecans

In a small bowl combine the oatmeal and water. Set aside. Preheat the oven to 350 degrees. In a large bowl combine the sugars, eggs, and oil. Add the oats/water mixture, flour, baking soda, cinnamon, and salt. Mix well. Pour into a greased and floured 9-by-13-inch baking pan. Bake for 35 minutes. Turn off the oven and leave the cake in the oven while making the icing. Combine the butter, milk, and brown sugar in a saucepan. Bring to a boil and boil for 1 minute. Add the pecans. Gently spread the icing over hot cake.

In addition to *Shoot/Don't Shoot*, J.A. Jance is the author of *Rattlesnake Crossing* and *Skeleton Canyon*.

Yankee Cake

EARLENE FOWLER

*T*his recipe has been in my family for forty years. It was the favorite cake of my mother, Mary Arnell, and has always been made best by her only sister, my aunt Florene. I mention the cake in my fifth book, *Dove in the Window*, when Benni is taking it to the annual Ramsey Ranch barbecue. The cake recipe isn't the only thing I stole from my mother's family for my books. Benni's last name, Harper, is also the maiden name of my maternal grandma, Muriel Sue, and Benni's first name comes from my cousin Benny, who is as different from the fictional Benni as can be. He's six feet tall and a fire chief for the Phoenix Fire Department.

In this cake I have used pecans (very Southern) and strawberry jam ('cause I always have this kind). But since it's a fruit/spice-type cake, I don't think it really matters.

2 cups sugar	1 cup fruit juice
1 cup butter, softened	1 cup buttermilk
1 teaspoon vanilla	4 eggs
3 ½ cups flour	1 cup jam
1 teaspoon baking soda	1 cup raisins
1 teaspoon allspice	1 cup nuts
1 teaspoon nutmeg	1 cup dates
1 teaspoon cinnamon	2 apples, cut into small pieces
1 teaspoon cloves	

Preheat the oven to 350 degrees.

In a large mixing bowl, blend the sugar, butter, and vanilla. Add the flour, baking soda, and the four spices. Beat in the juice, milk, and eggs. Fold in the jam, raisins, nuts, dates, and apples.

Divide the mixture into 3 or 4 greased 9-inch pans. Bake until a toothpick comes out clean (about 30 to 45 minutes, depending on your oven and the thickness of your layers). When cool, stack and frost with caramel frosting.

Frosting

4 tablespoons butter	⅔ cup whipping cream or evaporated milk
1 ⅓ cups packed brown sugar	5 cups powdered sugar
Salt to taste	1 teaspoon vanilla

Heat the butter in a saucepan until melted. Stir in the brown sugar, salt, and whipping cream. Heat to boiling, stirring constantly to keep from burning. Remove from heat and cool to lukewarm. Stir in the powdered sugar gradually, until the icing is thin enough to spread. Stir in the vanilla.

Earlene Fowler's mysteries take their titles from traditional quilt patterns and include *Dove in the Window* and *Mariner's Compass*.

Connie Collyer's Apple Cake

VALERIE S. MALMONT

*M*y second Tori Miracle mystery, *Death, Lies, and Apple Pies*, is set in rural Pennsylvania, and much of the action takes place at a country apple-butter festival. While Tori is visiting friends in the small community, she is asked to be the "celebrity" judge of the apple recipe contest. She is soon overwhelmed by hundreds of submissions. Her attempt to taste every entry ends when one of the pies is found to contain arsenic. (Don't worry—this is not *that* recipe!) For fun, I included the winning recipe for Applesauce-Oatmeal Cookies in the book.

The following recipe was served at a monthly book-discussion group I've belonged to for the past fifteen years. It was absolutely delicious and, best of all, simple to make. I asked our hostess, Marion Evans, if she would share the recipe. She said she'd be delighted to pass it on but wanted the credit to be given to the late Connie Collyer, who was an outstanding cook and friend. That's why I call this wonderful dessert Connie Collyer's Apple Cake.

> 3 cups flour
> 1 teaspoon baking soda
> 1 teaspoon salt
> 2 cups sugar
> 1 ½ cups oil
> 3 eggs
> 2 teaspoons vanilla
> ½ teaspoon *each*: nutmeg, cinnamon, and mace
> 1 cups raisins
> 1 cup walnuts
> 2 cups peeled, chopped apples

Mix together the flour, baking soda, and salt. Stir in the remaining ingredients and mix with a wooden spoon. Pour into a greased, floured Bundt pan. Bake 1 hour at 350 degrees. Cool 10 minutes, put on a plate, and poke about 30 holes in cake. Pour the warm glaze over the cake.

Glaze

Mix ½ stick of butter, ½ cup of brown sugar, and ⅛ cup of milk in a pan and bring to a boil. Cool slightly and pour over the cake.

Valerie S. Malmont's Tori Miracle series includes *Death Pays the Rose Rent* and *Death, Lies, and Apple Pies*.

Helen's Coconut Cake

PHYLLIS RICHMAN

*T*his recipe isn't new: It was my mother's. It isn't unpublished: I wrote a Mother's Day story about it. But it is one of my favorites, a recipe without which my family could not have a celebration.

As for its mystery significance:

1) It's a killer.

2) It always sets us in search of who ate the irresistible crunchy coconut topping without the cake. It is a family rule that you must eat it in proper proportion.

3) Although everyone in the family uses the same recipe, a really canny sleuth can tell by looking, smelling, and tasting exactly which of us made the one under consideration. Nobody made it as well as my mother.

4) The title of the recipe makes it pretty obvious how I named one of the most sympathetic characters in the newsroom of the *Examiner*, where Chas Wheatley is restaurant critic.

And let me warn you: Don't make this recipe unless you are having a party. Otherwise you will eat the whole thing and regret it.

> 1 cup milk
> 2 tablespoons butter, plus extra for the pan
> 4 eggs
> 2 cups sugar
> 2 cups sifted flour, plus extra for the pan
> 2 teaspoons baking powder
> ¼ teaspoon salt

For the Topping

> 6 tablespoons butter
> 10 tablespoons brown sugar
> 4-ounce can shredded Southern-style (not flaked) coconut
> 1 tablespoon vanilla

In a small saucepan, heat 1 cup milk with 2 tablespoons of butter to scalding. In the meantime, start beating 4 eggs in an electric mixer. Add the sugar and beat well until thick and foamy. With the beater going slow, gradually add the hot milk.

Sift the flour with the baking powder and salt. Beat into the egg mixture with the mixer on slow speed. Pour into a greased and floured 13-by-9-inch pan. Bake at 350 degrees for about 30 minutes, testing with a toothpick after 25 minutes to see if it is done. (Note: If your oven temperature tends to be low, bake at 375 degrees.) Let cool slightly in the pan.

To make the topping, melt 6 tablespoons of butter and add 10 tablespoons of brown sugar. Stir in the coconut and vanilla. Note: Use canned coconut, since it tends to be more moist than coconut packaged in bags. And Southern-style shredded coconut makes a crunchier topping than flaked coconut.

Spread the topping over the cake as evenly as possible. Put under the broiler about 4 to 6 inches below the heat, and broil until the topping is bubbling and brown. Turn the cake if necessary to brown it evenly, and broil until the topping is as brown as you can get it without burning it. Watch very carefully, as it turns from done to burned in an instant.

Let the cake cool, cut into squares, and serve. Put the squares in cupcake papers for serving if you wish.

Phyllis Richman, food writer for the *Washington Post*, is the author of *The Butter Did It: A Gastronomic Tale of Love and Murder*, the first in the Chas Wheatley series and its follow-up, *Murder on the Gravy Train*.

Sour Cream Cake

JOANNE DOBSON

*H*ere's the recipe for the sour cream coffee cake Karen Pelletier feeds Lieutenant Piotrowski in the wee hours of New Year's Day in *Quieter Than Sleep*.

Cake

1 cup butter
2 cups sugar
2 eggs
1 cup sour cream
½ teaspoon vanilla
2 cups flour
1 teaspoon baking powder
¼ teaspoon salt

Filling

4 teaspoons sugar
1 teaspoon cinnamon
1 cup chopped pecans or walnuts

Preheat the oven to 350 degrees. Grease and flour a tube pan.

First cream the butter and sugar until fluffy; beat the eggs in one at a time, then fold in the sour cream and vanilla. Sift the flour with baking powder and salt, and fold into the butter mixture.

Place about half of the batter in the pan. Mix all the filling ingredients together, then sprinkle ⅔ onto the batter in pan. Spoon the remaining batter in, and sprinkle the remaining nut mixture on top. Bake for 60 minutes; test with a toothpick (will be a little moist). Remove from the oven and cool on a rack.

This cake is lethal—but delicious.

Joanne Dobson's academic mysteries include *Quieter than Sleep* and *The Northbury Papers*.

Death by Chocolate

THE MYSTERY CAFÉ

A delectable triple threat—er, treat—of chocolate, this cake was a favorite at the Mystery Café. It has never been known to cause *serious* harm to anyone.

2 large eggs
¾ cup vegetable oil
¾ cup warm water
8 ounces sour cream
1 package devil's food cake mix
1 small package *instant* chocolate fudge pudding
1 12-ounce package chocolate chips
Confectioners' sugar

Combine the eggs, oil, water, and sour cream. Beat well. Add the cake mix and pudding. Beat until smooth. Fold in the chips.

Pour into a greased Bundt pan and bake at 350 degrees for 45 minutes or until wooden toothpick inserted in the center comes out clean.

Let cool in the pan on a cake rack for 15 minutes. Invert onto the rack and cool completely. Slide onto a plate and sprinkle the top with confectioners' sugar.

Serves 8.

Death by Chocolate 2

(If Three Chocolates Are Not Enough, Try This Lethal Variation)

Same cake ingredients as page 186.

Combine the eggs, oil, water, and sour cream. Beat well. Add the cake mix and only ½ package of the pudding. Beat until smooth. Fold in the chips.

Divide the batter between 2 greased 9-inch round cake pans. Bake for 40 minutes at 350 degrees or until a wooden toothpick inserted in the center comes out clean.

Cool the cake on racks for 15 minutes. Invert onto the racks and cool completely. Place 1 layer on a plate.

Pudding Filling

Prepare ½ package of the instant chocolate fudge pudding (left from cake ingredients) per package instructions, cutting measurements by half.

Spread pudding on top of the cake layer on the plate. For an added touch, sliced fresh raspberries or some all-fruit raspberry jam may be added on top of the pudding.

Place the second layer on the top. Spread Bittersweet Hard Icing (recipe below) on top and drizzle down the sides while still warm. If using the raspberries between layers, decorate the top with whole raspberries.

Since this cake is so chocolate-rich, a thin slice will more than satisfy even the most addicted chocaholic. Hence, depending on the dose of "poison" desired, this cake will serve up to 16!

Bittersweet Hard Icing

    4 tablespoons sweet butter
    2 ounces semisweet chocolate
    2 ounces unsweetened chocolate
    3 tablespoon heavy cream
    ⅔ cup sifted confectioners' sugar
    1 teaspoon vanilla

Melt the butter and chocolate over simmering water (in a double boiler), whisking constantly. Remove from heat and whisk in the cream. Add the sugar and vanilla. Whisk until smooth. Coat the top of the cake and drizzle the remaining icing down the sides.

Yield:1 ¼ cups.

Nicole's Kentucky Bourbon Cake

GRANT MICHAELS

*N*icole Albright, resident manicurist and secret owner of Snips Salon, says about this recipe:

> *"As a quiet child in rural Kentucky I used to help my old gran' make this cake every year. I have fond memories of her showing me how to break the big Georgia pecans into four equal pieces, and how to scrape the bowl so clean even the cat had nothing to lick. Later, when I was a model in Paris, I used to make it for my friends, who adored it. I had to watch my weight, of course, so I could have only a crumb or two myself. Still, the bourbon was always excellent."*

This large holiday cake is a spiked and spicy pound cake with fruit and nuts. It's nothing at all like a typical sticky fruitcake. It does require a little planning, but raves and inebriation are guaranteed.

1 pound candied red cherries	1 bottle good Kentucky bourbon
½ pound pitted dates	

Ahead-of-time prep: Cut the cherries in half; rinse in hot water and drain. Cut the dates in halves or thirds. Mix the 2 fruits in a bowl, and pour in enough bourbon to cover. Seal the bowl and soak the fruits for 2 *weeks*; stir occasionally and add bourbon as needed to keep everything covered.

1 pound pecans, broken into large pieces	1 cup white sugar
5 cups sifted all-purpose flour	9 large eggs, separated
¾ pound unsalted butter	1 teaspoon baking powder
1 cup brown sugar	2 teaspoons nutmeg

Preheat the oven to 275 degrees. Drain the cherries and dates; save the bourbon! Coat the nuts with a bit of flour. Cream the butter with sugar. Add yolks one at a time and beat well. Mix ½ cup of flour with the baking soda and nutmeg; set aside. Sift the remaining flour into the batter, alternating with the reserved bourbon. Add the nutmeg flour after all the other flour is in batter. Fold in the cherries and dates, then the nuts. Beat the egg whites until stiff, then fold into the batter.

Pour into a large buttered and floured tube pan or Pullman loaf pan. Bake at 275 degrees for at least 2 hours, or until a skewer comes out clean. Cool the cake completely on a wire rack, then wrap it in bourbon-drenched cheesecloth. Seal in foil and store in a cool place for up to a month, rewetting the cheesecloth with bourbon as needed.

Slice thin and serve at room temperature.

Note: If you make the cake in a Pullman loaf, you can cut gift-sized chunks for your best, best friends.

Grant Michaels' hairstylist-sleuth, Stan Kraychik, first appeared in *A Body to Dye For.* Some of his more recent escapades may be found in *Dead as a Doornail* and *Time To Check Out.*

Aunt Zell's Pecan Pie

MARGARET MARON

*I*n *Bootlegger's Daughter*, Deborah and her cousin Reed are eating lunch at Sue's Soup 'n' Sandwich Shop when the subject of pie comes up:

> *"How 'bout a nice slice of pie?" asked our waitress as she paused at our booth to top off our cups with more coffee. "We've got deep-dish apple or there's one piece of pecan left."*
>
> *Pecan pie's my absolute favorite and I do indulge in the wintertime—after all, what are bulky sweaters for?—but good as Sue's is, it doesn't hold a candle to my Aunt Zell's and I don't squander those five hundred calories on anybody else's.*
>
> *"I'll take the apple," said Reed, who wore a bulky red sweater vest under his gray tweed sportscoat.*
>
> *I was wearing a cropped green jacket over a soft challis skirt that registered every ounce I ate, so I passed.*

Here's Zell's recipe:

> 3 eggs, separated
> ½ cup sugar
> 1 cup dark corn syrup
> 2 tablespoons melted margarine
> 1 teaspoon vanilla
> Dash of salt
> 2 cups chopped pecans
> ½ cup pecan halves
> 1 9-inch deep-dish pastry shell

Using clean beaters and bowl (no oily film), beat the egg whites till stiff and set aside.

Beat the egg yolks till frothy. Add the next 5 ingredients till well-blended. Add chopped nuts. Gently fold the batter into the egg whites, taking care to mix, but not break down, the egg whites.

Pour into a deep-dish pastry shell. Arrange the pecan halves in a pattern around the edge. Bake at 350 degrees for 50 to 55 minutes or until a knife inserted halfway between the center and the edge comes out clean. ("Mind you don't overbake it," says Aunt Zell.)

Delicious hot or cold, plain, or with a dollop of whipped cream or vanilla ice cream.

Among Margaret Maron's many mysteries is the Judge Deborah Knot series, which includes Edgar winner *Bootlegger's Daughter*, *Shooting at Loons*, and *The Home Fires*.

Valerie Wilson Wesley's Apple Pie

VALERIE WILSON WESLEY

I—and probably my character Tamara Hayle—love a good apple pie. My two daughters request this every Thanksgiving, and I've tried to present it here as accurately as I can. If I'm in a sour mood, I use a little more sugar. If I'm feeling sweet, I add more cinnamon. Good cooking is like good jazz—each dish is a little bit different each time you make it. Hope you enjoy this one.

> 1 ready-made pie crust (who has time to actually make a crust!)
> 8 peeled and sliced Cortland and Granny Smith apples
>   (variety is the spice of life)
> ¾ cup blended dark and white sugar
>   (if the apples are very sweet, use less)
> 1 teaspoon cinnamon
> 1 teaspoon nutmeg
> 1 teaspoon vanilla (to add some flavah!)
> 2 tablespoons cornstarch (to thicken juices)
> Juice of 1 lemon
> Unsalted butter
> Milk or egg yolks to wash

Preheat the oven to 425 degrees. It will be turned down to 350 degrees.

Place the bottom layer of pie crust in a pie plate. Toss the apples together with the other ingredients until they are nicely coated. Put the apples into the bottom crust. Dot very generously with butter. Squeeze a bit of lemon juice over them. Cover with the top crust. Prepare for baking by fluting the edges and making decorative slashes so that steam can escape. Brush the crust lightly with milk or egg yolks to give it a nice glaze. Place in the hot, 425-degree oven for about 15 minutes, then turn the oven down to 350 degrees and let it bake until nicely browned.

Valerie Wilson Wesley is the author of the Tamara Hayle mystery series, which includes *Easier to Kill, No Hiding Place,* and *Devil's Gonna Get Him.*

Mom Hayter's Apple Pie

SPARKLE HAYTER

*T*his is the best apple pie I've ever had, perfect for eating with vanilla ice cream and a cup of spiked coffee by the fire while reading my books or plotting how to do in that arsehole next door.

Double Crust

1 pound extra sharp aged cheddar
½ cup shortening
2 ¾ cups all-purpose flour
1 teaspoon salt
6 to 7 tablespoons cold water

First grate the cheddar in a food processor. Add the shortening and process until well-blended. Put in the refrigerator for half an hour.

Spoon the flour into a measuring cup and level. Combine the flour and salt in a medium bowl.

Cut in the cheddar/shortening blend using a pastry blender (or 2 knives) until all the flour is blended to form pea-size chunks. Sprinkle with water, 1 tablespoon at a time. Toss lightly with a fork until the dough will form a ball. Refrigerate for 15 minutes to make rolling easier. Divide into 2 balls and roll out.

Filling

5 to 6 large Granny Smith apples
¾ cup golden brown sugar
1 tablespoon lemon juice

Peel and slice the apples into a pastry-lined pie pan. Sprinkle the sugar and lemon juice on top. Cover with the top crust. Poke the top crust with a fork in a few spots to vent the steam. Bake at 425 degrees for 10 minutes, then reduce to 325 degrees and bake for 35 minutes more. The cheddar in this crust sometimes makes it crumbly, but it's delicious.

Sparkle Hayter, herself a former CNN reporter, has created journalist-sleuth Robin Hudson, who appears in *The Last Manly Man*.

Mama (Candi Covington) Sweet Potato Pie
NORA DELOACH

Grace Covington, nicknamed Candi because of a golden brown complexion that looks like candied sweet potatoes, is a case manager for the country's welfare department. She is also an exceptional cook. Candi's real passion, however, is sleuthing. Here's a taste of her culinary skills.

3 eggs, slightly beaten
3 cups cooked, mashed sweet potatoes
⅔ cup evaporated milk
⅓ cup whipping cream
1 cup sugar
1 teaspoon vanilla
½ teaspoon salt
½ teaspoon cinnamon
¼ teaspoon ground nutmeg
½ teaspoon ground ginger
1 unbaked (10-inch) pie shell
¼ cup butter or margarine, softened
½ cup firmly packed brown sugar
½ cup chopped pecans

Combine the eggs, sweet potatoes, milk, cream, sugar, vanilla, salt, and spices. Blend well. Pour the mixture into the pie shell. Bake at 350 degrees for 40 to 50 minutes or until the filling is set.

Combine the butter and ½ cup of brown sugar. Blend well. Stir in the pecans. Sprinkle the mixture on the pie. Bake at 350 degrees for 10 minutes.

Nora DeLoach is the author of *Mama Stalks the Past*, *Mama Solves a Murder* and *Mama Rocks the Empty Cradle*.

Mae's Louisiana Kitchen Sweet Potato Pie

ROBERT GREER

*T*his pie is a staple of CJ Floyd, my African-American bail-bondsman protagonist. CJ's love interest, Mavis Sundee, owns a soul-food restaurant, where he spends far too much time sampling the fare.

> *When he was thirteen, on an early-fall day, his uncle had sent him pedaling his JC Higgins from the office to Mae's to pick up two catfish-and-collard dinners and a sweet potato pie.*
>
> *Mavis, who had seen him ride up and whose head barely cleared the counter-top, rang him out at the cash register and asked him how he planned to balance his dinners and a sweet potato pie while pedaling home. Somehow he managed, but it was another thirty years before he and Mavis were able to balance their own relationship.*

> —from *The Devil's Red Nickel*

2 pounds cooked sweet potatoes
½ stick butter (optional)
3 large eggs
⅓ cup white sugar
⅓ cup brown sugar
1 ½ teaspoons ground cinnamon
½ teaspoon ground nutmeg
½ teaspoon salt
1 tablespoon vanilla
1 tablespoon lemon juice
¾ cup heavy cream
¾ cup half-and-half
1 purchased 9-inch pie crust

Preheat the oven to 350 degrees. Place the cooked sweet potatoes in the bowl of an electric mixer and whip until smooth. Whip in the butter, eggs, and all the other ingredients until fluffy. Pour the filling into the crust. Bake until the filling is puffed at edges and just set in center, about 40 minutes.

Serves 8.

Robert Greer's mystery novels featuring CJ Floyd include *The Devil's Hatband*, *The Devil's Red Nickel* and *The Devil's Backbone*.

Winner's Circle Pie

SARAH R. SHABER

*T*his is a delicious pie, if I say so myself. My mother gave me the recipe, but I don't know where she got it. Aficionados of Southern cooking will quickly deduce that it is closely related to the famous Kentucky Derby pie. The recipe can be tripled, and the pie freezes very successfully for up to three months. I give these pies as Christmas presents every year. Once, a friend of mine, upon hearing that I had dropped a pie off at her house, left work and drove home for a slice!

    ¼ cup butter, softened
    1 cup sugar
    3 eggs, beaten
    ¾ cup light corn syrup
    2 tablespoons bourbon
    ¼ teaspoon salt
    1 teaspoon vanilla
    ½ cup semisweet chocolate chips
    ½ to ¾ cup chopped pecans
    1 packaged pie shell

Preheat the oven to 375 degrees. Cream the butter until fluffy. Add the sugar gradually and continue to beat. Add the beaten eggs. Add all the other ingredients and mix well. Pour into the pie shell and bake at 375 degrees until the pie is brown and set, approximately 30 to 40 minutes. Cool and enjoy!

Sarah R. Shaber made her debut with *Simon Said.*

Vinegar Pie

DEBORAH K. ADAMS

*J*esus Creek, Tennessee, is really the central character in my cozy mysteries in which the main characters in one are likely to show up as minor characters in another. This pie is always a big favorite at Jesus Creek potlucks.

> ¼ cup butter
> 2 cups sugar
> ½ teaspoon cloves
> Dash of salt
> Dash of cinnamon
> 4 eggs, separated
> 2 to 3 tablespoons cider vinegar
> 9-inch pie crust (homemade—don't even think
>   about using one of those frozen things)

Preheat the oven to 425 degrees.

Cream the butter and sugar, then add spices and blend well. Beat in the yolks with a beater until smooth and creamy. Add the vinegar and beat again until the mixture is smooth. Beat the egg whites with salt until they stiffen, then fold into the sugar mixture.

Pour into the pie crust and bake 15 minutes at 425 degrees, then reduce the heat to 300 degrees and bake another 20 minutes. When done, the top should be nicely brown and the center of the pie should come out dry when poked with a knife.

Macavity Award-winner Deborah K. Adams' first novel, *All the Great Pretenders*, was nominated for the Agatha Award. Her other titles include *All the Blood Relations*, *All the Deadly Beloved* and *All the Hungry Mothers*.

Dieting-Is-Murder Cheesecake

BETH SHERMAN

$\mathcal{N}$ either my sleuth, Anne Hardaway, nor I cook. We both would rather eat fast food (preferably greasy and cheap). But on those rare occasions when we have something to celebrate, like the publication of my first novel, *Dead Man's Float*, we like to whip up this pie. It's easy to make (crucial for nonbakers), mouthwateringly good, and guaranteed to impress our friends. ("Hey, she writes *and* cooks!"). Plus, there are delicious bowls to lick.

And it gives us a great sugar rush when we're both trying to figure out how the heck so many people wind up dead in a tiny Jersey shore town (population 703 and dwindling rapidly).

Pie Shell

> 1 stick butter
> 1 ½ cups graham crackers (about 18 to 20)
> 3 tablespoons sugar
> Dash of cinnamon

Melt the butter and then mix with graham-cracker crumbs, sugar and cinnamon. Evenly pack the bottom and sides of a 9-inch pie pan.

Filling

> 4 eggs
> ½ cup sugar
> 1 teaspoon vanilla
> 4 3-ounce packages cream cheese, softened

Preheat the oven to 375 degrees. Using an electric mixer, beat the eggs until they are lemon-colored. Add the sugar and beat well. Add the vanilla and cream cheese; beat until smooth and creamy. Pour into the pie shell. Bake at 375 degrees for 20 minutes or until set like custard. Remove from the oven and cool on a rack for 10 minutes.

Topping

> 1 cup sour cream
> 4 tablespoons sugar
> 1 teaspoon vanilla

Turn the oven up to 400 degrees. While the pie is cooling, mix the sour cream, sugar and vanilla. Spread evenly over the pie. Return the pie to the oven and bake at 400 degrees for 8 minutes. Remove and cool on a rack.

Chill before serving.

Beth Sherman has spent most of her career as a newspaper reporter and decorating columnist. *Dead Man's Float* is her first mystery novel.

Grandma Grover's Cream Puffs

(as devoured in *Just Desserts*)

MARY DAHEIM

This recipe comes from the files of my cousin, Judith Marshall Collins, who inspired my Bed and Breakfast heroine, Judith McMonigle Flynn. The recipe was handed down to Judith by our grandmother, Mary Dawson, and we figure it's almost a hundred years old. Thus, we can be sure that Grandma Dawson made these cream puffs on a woodstove while she lived in the real logging town of Alpine, Washington, from 1915 to 1920. My mother, Monica Dawson Richardson, may also have baked these cream puffs during the early years of her marriage in Alpine, circa 1926-27, shortly before the mill was closed and the town was razed.

Cream Puff Shells

½ cup butter
1 cup boiling water
1 cup bread flour
4 unbeaten eggs

Add the butter to the water. Heat until the butter melts. Add the flour all at once and stir vigorously until a ball forms in the center of the pan. Remove from fire. Add eggs one at a time, beating one at a time.

The mixture should be very stiff. Shape on a buttered cookie sheet by dropping from a spoon. Bake 40 to 60 minutes at 375 degrees, until free from beads of moisture.

Cream Puff Filling

1 cup sugar
½ teaspoon salt
¾ cups flour
2 eggs, beaten
2 cups milk
1 teaspoon vanilla
Whipping cream

Mix the sugar, salt, and flour. Stir in the well-beaten eggs. Heat the milk to the boiling point—don't boil. Stir into the mixture. Put in a double boiler and cook until thick, stirring constantly. When almost cool, add the vanilla. To thicken, add whipping cream until desired consistency is reached.

Frosting

2 ounces unsweetened chocolate
1 cup sugar
3 tablespoons cornstarch
1 cup boiling water
2 tablespoons butter, cut up
1 tablespoon vanilla
¼ teaspoon salt

Melt the chocolate in a saucepan over low heat. Add the sugar and cornstarch. Mix well, then slowly stir in the boiling water. Cook and stir until thick and smooth. Add the butter, vanilla, and salt. Beat thoroughly.

When cooled, slice the cream puff shell in half, side to side. Place a large dollop of the filling on the bottom half of the cream puff. Replace the top half, pressing it lightly in place. Drip the frosting freely over the top, allowing it to drip down the sides. (If doing each one on an individual plate, allow the sauce to run onto the plate. Garnish with a sprig of mint.)

Makes 10 servings.

Judith McMonigle Flynn, Mary Daheim's Bed and Breakfast heroine, can be found in *Just Desserts* and others; her Emma Lord mysteries include *The Alpine Kindred* and *The Alpine Icon*.

Wardens in Wine

PETER LOVESEY

The favorite dish of my Victorian detective, Bertie, Prince of Wales, was ptarmigan pie. Unfortunately (well, fortunately for the ptarmigan), the ptarmigan is now a protected bird, and if I supplied the recipe I would risk being arrested and having this cookbook produced as evidence. Instead, here's a tasty dessert from an earlier book called *On the Edge* about two women in 1946 who decide to murder their husbands. The recently widowed Rose is preparing a meal for Hector, her friend's husband.

> *There was a story her mother delighted in telling about the evening Daddy had thrown his annual dinner part at the rectory for the church wardens and their wives. It had always been a staid affair. That year Mummy had found a recipe for pears poached in red wine which proved to be such a success that two or three of the guest had become merry after their second helpings. When they'd all tottered out at the end of the evening, Daddy had asked what the recipe was called. Mummy had given him an innocent smile and said, "Wardens in Wine." A warden, she'd discovered, was an old English name for a pear used in cooking.*
>
> *She'd noticed several bottles of Burgundy lying on their sides on the floor of the larder. If there were any pears left on the greengrocer's stall, her problem would be solved. Although it was almost dark, the man was still there, working under an electric light bulb. Rose bought three large Comice pears. Twenty-five past five. Ten minutes' preparation and twenty for poaching. She could just get everything done in time.*

Zest of 1 orange	6 cloves
1 pint red Burgundy wine	6 Comice pears*
8 ounces castor sugar	

*Genuine wardens—or cooking pears—are difficult to find and less delicious than the Comice variety, so I recommend the latter.

Take the zest from the orange and cut it into the finest strips.

Slowly boil the wine, sugar, cloves, and zest into a syrup, ensuring that the sugar is fully dissolved.

Peel and quarter the pears and remove the cores. Pour the syrup over them, first removing the cloves. Ensure that the pears are fully immersed.

Cook in the oven at 400 degrees until tender.

Serve warm or chilled.

Peter Lovesey has written more than twenty mysteries, including his series featuring Victorian Sergeant Cribb. His new award-winning series about contemporary police detective Peter Diamond includes *Bloodhounds*, *The Summons* and *Upon a Dark Night*.

Strong Poison Sweet Omelette

The final course was a sweet omelette, which was made at the table in a chafing-dish by Philip Boyes himself. Both Mr. Urquhart and his cousin were very particular about eating an omelette the moment it came from the pan—and a very good rule it is, and I advise you to treat omelettes in the same way and never to allow them to stand, or they will get tough....

Philip Boyes then...himself divided it into two portions, giving one to Mr. Urquhart and taking the remainder himself.

Now, how is it that Philip Boyes has been poisoned and not Mr. Urquhart? The solution to Dorothy L. Sayers' classic *Strong Poison*— and the life of Harriet Vane—may or may not depend on this perplexing detail.

    4 eggs
    Sugar
    1 tablespoon butter
    ⅓ cup jam of your choice, warmed

Break the eggs into a bowl and beat with a whisk or fork. Beat in the sugar. Over high heat, melt the butter in an omelette pan. Pour in the eggs so that they completely cover the bottom of the pan.

When the eggs begin to grow firm, spread the warmed jam in the center. Fold the omelette over on itself. Turn the omelette out onto a warm plate, sprinkle with additional sugar if desired.

Serves 2.

Denouement Apple/Pear Crisp
KATHERINE HALL PAGE

This recipe from the kitchen of Faith Fairchild can be made with pears or apples. It is especially delicious with a mixture of apples, such as Empire or Delicious (sweets) and Macoun or McIntosh (slightly tart).

> 1 ¾ to 2 pounds apples or pears
> Juice of ½ lemon
> 2 tablespoons maple syrup
> ¾ cup flour
> ¼ teaspoon salt
> 3 teaspoons brown sugar
> 6 tablespoons unsalted butter

Peel, core, and slice the fruit. Toss it in a bowl with the lemon juice to prevent browning.

Place the slices in a lightly buttered baking dish. Drizzle with the maple syrup.

Put the flour, salt, sugar, and butter in the bowl of a food processor fitted with a metal blade, and process briefly. You may also cut the butter with a pastry cutter or 2 knives. The mixture should be crumbly. Cover the fruit evenly with the flour mixture and bake in a preheated 375-degree oven for 45 minutes or until the juices are bubbling.

Let sit for 5 minutes and serve with whipped cream, vanilla ice cream, or crème fraîche.

Faith Fairchild is featured in Katherine Hall Page's New England-based series, including *The Body in the Bouillon, The Body in the Kelp* and *The Body in the Bookcase.*

Apricot Dessert

ANNETTE MEYERS

$\mathcal{H}$ere's my favorite summer dessert recipe, but I've never given it a title. I don't know. Maybe: Apricot Dessert. It's not exactly a compote and not exactly a stew, but you can call it Apricot Compote if you like.

For the best taste, this dessert can only be made in the summer, when the local apricots are being picked and presented at farmers' markets.

Also, since I don't use exact measures (and you don't have to for this), it's fairly simple to make.

> 1 to 1 ½ pounds really fresh summer apricots (not supermarket quality
>   if at all possible)
> 1 to 2 teaspoons granulated sugar
> 1 teaspoon pure vanilla extract

Pit the apricots and leave them in halves. Place the halved apricots in a heavy pot (I use Creusetware). Sprinkle with the sugar and vanilla; toss well. Allow to macerate for 1 hour, tossing several times. Cover with a tight lid and sweat the apricots over low heat for 20 to 25 minutes, until they begin to fall apart. Remove from heat and uncover.

Serve warm or cold (best is at room temperature) with a scoop of plain nonfat yogurt and topped generously with toasted sliced almonds.

Annette Meyers' Smith and Wetzen mysteries include *The Groaning Board* and *These Bones were Made for Dancin'*. With her husband, Martin, she writes historical mysteries set in New York in the seventeenth, eighteenth, and nineteenth centuries under the name Maan Meyers, and their books include *The Lucifer Contract* and *The House on Mulberry Street*.

Scotch Trifle

(The Royal Favorite)

ALANNA KNIGHT

*I*n *To Kill A Queen*, Inspector Faro is about to enjoy his favorite dish, Royal Salmon. However, his plate was too quickly taken from him. *Resentfully he saw that the Queen was drumming her fingers on the tablecloth, impatiently awaiting her own particular favourite, Scotch Trifle.*

Plain sponge cake
1 schooner sherry*
1 ½ cups raspberry jelly
Small tin of fruit (peaches, apricots, or cocktail assortment),
    juice separated
2 cups custard
1 cup whipping cream

Soak the sponge cake in the sherry. Mix the jelly and fruit juice; pour over the sponge cake and allow to set. Stir the fruit into the custard and pour over the cake. Add the whipped cream on top before serving.

Note from the author: This is a great way to use up a sponge cake that may have dried out a bit. Start by tearing it into pieces and placing them in a deep dish. Then continue with the recipe as above.

*Helpful hint: A schooner is a British measure equal to 14 ounces.

Scottish author Alanna Knight's Victorian Edinburgh policeman, Jeremy Faro, appears in such books as *The Coffin Lane Murders, Scottish Feast* and *To Kill a Queen.*

Pêche Melba

CAROLA DUNN

*I*n my Daisy Dalrymple mystery, *Styx and Stones*, when Daisy's brother-in-law recommends the oysters Rockefeller in a month with no *R*, Daisy knows trouble's on the way. She orders consommé madrilène instead, followed by sole Colbert, chicken Mireille, and pêche Melba. Ah, they knew how to eat in the twenties!

Vanilla Syrup

1 ¼ cups sugar
1 quart water
1 vanilla bean (or 1 teaspoon vanilla essence)
Zest of 1 lemon (outer peel thinly peeled)

Simmer together (or microwave), stirring occasionally till all the sugar is dissolved.

Poach the peaches in syrup over low heat until tender but not soft. Cool in syrup, skin, halve, and remove stone. Refrigerate.

Raspberry Puree

1 pint raspberries
3 tablespoons sugar
2 teaspoons strained lemon juice

Simmer together till soft, then sieve out the seeds.

To serve: Place the peach halves upside down on a scoop of vanilla ice cream in individual bowls (for easier serving) and top with the raspberry puree.

Too, too heavenly, says Daisy.

Carola Dunn has written around thirty Regencies and six Daisy Dalrymple mysteries set in England in the 1920s, including *Styx and Stones*, *Murder of the Flying Scotsman* and *Damsel in Distress*.

Index

Jo Grossman is the former proprietor of The Mystery Café, a mystery bookstore/café that combined her love of good food and good crime novels, in Sheffield, Massachusetts. She worked in film and television for many years, including a three-year stint on *In the Heat of the Night*.

Robert Weibezahl is a writer and publicist. A monthly book review columnist for *BookPage*, his articles on books and culture have also appeared in *Mystery Readers Journal*, *Irish America* magazine, the *Los Angeles Daily News*, the *Los Angeles Reader*, and the *Dictionary of Literary Biography Yearbook*. He lives in California.

To receive a free catalog of other Poisoned Pen Press titles, please contact us in one of the following ways:

Phone: 1-800-421-3976
Facsimile: 1-480-949-1707
Email: info@poisonedpenpress.com
Website: www.poisonedpenpress.com

Poisoned Pen Press
6962 E. First Ave. Ste 103
Scottsdale, AZ 85251